EYE OF THE HURRICANE

OREGON STATE MONOGRAPHS

Studies in Education and Guidance

CARVEL W. WOOD, *Consulting Editor*

EYE of the
HURRICANE

Observations on Creative
Educational Administration

Warren Barr Knox

Corvallis
Oregon State University Press

LB
2805
.K56

Library of Congress Cataloging in Publication Data

Knox, Warren Barr, 1925-
  Eye of the hurricane.

  (Oregon State monographs: Studies in education and guidance, 6)
  1. School management and organization. I. Title. II. Series.
LB2805.K56   371.2   73-4006
ISBN 0-87071-046-X

Printed in United States of America

To Nancy

Preface

THE KINGDOM OF ACADEMIA is here defined as that sometimes never-never land of education from kindergarten to graduate school. The chief administrative officer is, if nothing else, unique in his school, college, university, system, or district. There is only one of him, or her, to an institution. This fact may be viewed quite differently by various colleagues and constituencies, but it remains intrinsically the same.

The following collection of essays is an attempt to underline the potentially creative role or roles of the principal and the superintendent; of the president, the provost, and the chancellor. In addition to what is hoped will be a philosophical treatment of the problems and potentials of the institutional executive, some satirical fun is poked occasionally at the educational administrator. If we cannot always have a fifth and a sixth sense, enabling us to see around the corner, we can at least use or develop a seventh: a sense of humor— most pointed when it is pointed at ourselves.

This is not a collection of wisdoms or judgments. More often than not, a principal or a superintendent or a president finds his "wisdom" in the counsel of his colleagues; his judgments must be taken from sets of circumstances in which he variously sits at the prosecution or defense table, in the jury box, the witness chair, and the prisoner's dock. Only occasionally is he on the bench. The chief administrator's job is one that everyone knows he could do well yet no one wants. The man or woman who accepts it and who stays with it must be a strange combination of people within a person. A complete spectrumal spectre, made up of characteristics and attitudes which run concurrently and which vary from supreme confidence to abject fear. It is wise (there is that word again) that neither red nor violet be reflected in anything but one's own mirror.

The several thousands words which crowd these pages may be clarifying in some respects; they may only muddy the water in others. But it is hoped that there is something for everyone who now holds a chief educational administrative position or is contemplating the stages of doing so. There may even be something for those who would not have the job on a silver platter today, but who find themselves searching for the silver polish tomorrow.

At times critical and negative, these essays try, for the most part, to be encouraging and positive. The affirmative factors in American education and in the challenges and rewards for the educational unit leader need to be made visible as never before. Educational administration at all levels must be strong, positive, enduring, compassionate, firm, practical, and imaginative. These are not skills; they are human characteristics. From the abundant ranks of college and university students and from those young men and women who have recently begun careers in education, the field of administration must draw those who embody the essential combination of sensitivity, creativity, and the desire to lead. A long-held belief of the essayist is that while details and specifics of duties and responsibilities of administrative leaders from elementary school to the university are in many ways quite different, the essentials of leadership and philosophy and attitude and humanness are strikingly similar.

Finally, it is hoped that some of the thoughts, second thoughts, and reminders herein will be useful to members of boards of trustees, visitors, regents, and overseers, as well as to members of public school boards. Choosing and retaining a chief administrative officer, as voices from widely divergent sources continue to point out, are among their most serious obligations.

Contents

I. A Pathway to Somewhere

FEW PERSONS are privileged to be engaged in a career of *life influence*. Education provides one of the best examples of such a career and the chief executive of any educational institution or institutions, be he or she principal, superintendent, president, or chancellor, holds a position of leadership opportunity unique to the profession.

It is, of course, assumed that any eager and intelligent chief administrator-elect should be ready to accept his defined responsibilities as outlined by his board. He should be willing to defend and to foster the principles of sound educational practices and policies. He should be able to support and to initiate change when he believes it to be warranted and to be in the best interests of most in his charge.

But an administrative career should point one somewhere other than to the next upward rung on the pay ladder or to the next Monday morning at the desk. However difficult it is to verbalize and however impossible to write into a working description of responsibilities, the top man in any educational unit should be on a *pathway to somewhere* and should be able to convince his several constituencies to be on that pathway with him. This concept, I am certain, is more than a pathway of "institutional purpose" printed in college catalogs and in school district directives. It is much deeper than a personal "philosophy of education," which can periodically change within the person (many times for the betterment of the institution) but which is standard practice as a part of the pre-employment interview and considered to be a lifetime commitment.

The administrator in authority, and he or she alone, is in the unique and very personal position to understand and to move the total animal. And the opportunities for doing so are to be found not only in the thousand decisions of day-to-day institutional operation

11

or in the long-range planning and direction by which an institution looks to the future. They are to be found in the very heart and viscera of the institution itself and of the man himself. If this is true, and both observation and experience tells me that it is, then the life and future of the institution he has been selected to serve for a relatively small slice of time are singularly his own overwhelming responsibility. And the school or college or university is, finally, a very real reflection of the chief administrative officer and of his personal persuasions. None can tell him the magnitude of this responsibility prior to his assumption of it and, after it is assumed, those about him can only be compassionate, critical, or indifferent during its course. It must be experienced, and he alone can do that in his time and place. He can hope for a strong measure of understanding and a majority of support. But at the moment of decision he stands or falls by himself.

One of the realities of academic institutional life can be of assistance as the chief executive officer enters the center ring shouldering the challenges and responsibilities of ultimate leadership; as he carries with him, handcuffed to his wrist for twenty-four hours a day, the attaché case of problems, sorrows, accomplishments, joys, disappointments, and victories. It is the confidence in his own ability that automatically sets him on the pathway to somewhere—and the knowledge that those whom he serves *expect* him to be out in front.

Where Is Somewhere?

It is a great temptation to answer the question, "Where is somewhere?" with a simple, "Anywhere." But by so doing I am afraid that I would be on shaky philosophical ground and, further, that I would be almost universally misunderstood. To suggest that an institution set academic sail for *anywhere* is certain also to run up a red flag on the halyard. For faculties, boards, and the taxpaying and contributing citizenry are conditioned to approve and to pay for the specific and the definable and the obvious (the best way to cross Kansas in July is in a straight line). And so, with wistful reluctance, I will in passing only note that anywhere is usually better than nowhere, that a straight-line trip is only the *quickest* way to cross

Kansas in July, and hope that the point is partially made. We had better return to the term "somewhere" because it can be identified and, moreover, because "anywhere" has sadly ceased to carry a flavor of adventure and has instead taken on a connotation of confusion and nondirection. Perhaps we can please nearly everyone: "somewhere" still holds a degree of comfort for the cautious and the easily alarmed; it also retains some possibilities for adventure. And adventure is at the center of my concern.

The pathway to somewhere ought to be an adventure as broad and as long as individual and institutional imaginations can make it. It can have as many crooked lanes and corners and turns and blind alleys as a medieval city and as many discoveries, insights, and delights as a perpetual Renaissance. The *pathway* through Academia is of more importance to the traveler than the *somewhere* on the other side. The trip is of more importance than the destination. Indeed, the destination is, after all, of importance only in that it can shove a person or an institution off on a new pathway toward a new *somewhere*. Consider what comes to mind when we think of a pathway: meandering, not always easy to follow, often unmarked, resisting the traveler who is in a hurry, resenting the nonseeing and the single-minded. A pathway to somewhere, in the best tradition of educational purpose, is the antithesis of an academic freeway. A freeway can only offer controlled speed, controlled direction, and an appalling compulsion to get *there* with as few rest stops and as little sight-seeing as possible. Such is not adventure, and such is not education.

What of leadership and pathways? "This institution needs a leader who knows exactly where he's going." This is a time-honored and still popular way for presidential selection committees and searching school boards to phrase what they believe to be one of the primary requisites for educational leadership. Upon close inspection, this requirement *cannot* be primary; if it is, the institution will, in the long run, stand still. Let's attempt a rephrase: "This institution needs a leader who has strong and reasoned convictions about how he proposes to get to *somewhere* and who might have to wander all over the map before he gets there or who might have to change his mind about where *somewhere* is along the way." I suggest that this is what trustees and board members should be looking for if they really know their institutions and if they really care about education. And I am certain that if boards and administrators and teachers are convinced that speed is not to be equated with excellence, then they have another decision to make : Is the pathway of a wandering, deliberate adventure a better way to think of the process of education than a sterile, plodding progress toward a degree or a diploma? And, if it is, what sort of chief executive should be sought?

Any administrator in authority must be an adventurer and must recognize that leadership does not mean exercising authority over a parade route, a predetermined, lock-step march which begins at the city hall and ends up at the fairgrounds. That sort of trip does not need someone to lead ; it only requires someone to steer. A great deal of the time, despite "master plans," "goals for the future," and other adopted policies, institutions find themselves in the tall grass, if not in the jungle. This is not to say that the total life of a school or college is to be spent wandering about in the weeds, but the administrator who says he knows exactly where he and the school are going all of the time is naive, pompous, or foolish—or all three.

To break new trail, to stay as close to the resulting pathways as possible, and to keep an eye on the general direction of "somewhere" is the real challenge of the man or woman who sits in the Chair of Responsibility (sometimes referred to as the "hot seat" by a variety of constituents for a variety of reasons). Those who lead and would lead must be adventurers and they can never give a pat answer to the question "Where is somewhere?" If they can, the institutions or districts which they serve are, in the final sense, going *nowhere*. They have lost the meaning of the journey. They are missing the essential challenges and the abundant rewards of association with education-in-motion, with learning-in-purpose.

The process is of greater importance than the result; the search is more important than the discovery. It is not enough that boards and instructors realize these essentials; the top administrative officer must continuously remind them, encourage them, and stand as a personal example.

The Odyssey and the Individual

There can be no doubt that there exists a uniquely strong bond between the institution and the person in charge. This link is both philosophical and real, and it is overwhelming. It is also not easily defined or even fully understood. But the combination of leader and school is among the best examples in our society of a tremendous potential for power.

Let not the word *power,* as used here, be misunderstood. The ultimate legal power of any institution is, of course, vested in the same body as the ultimate legal responsibility—the lay board (directors, trustees, regents, overseers, visitors, or whatever the corporate structure provides). Power of that sort remains constant under the bylaws and the state law. Whether or not the exercise of that power is of high or lower order and whether or not any education takes place within or without its institutional walls and in its name is quite another consideration. True, the board transfers a great portion of the power to implement its purposes to the chief executive. In some instances, boards have shared this power of implementation with administration, faculty, and to an increasing degree, with students. No, I do not think I mean shared *power.* Perhaps a better term would be shared discussion and recommendation. Students are not faculty; administrators are not trustees; alumni are not legislators. If individuals in these clearly separate groups share the ultimate power and, in so doing, govern, then it seems to me they must give up their participation in decisions affecting those groups from which they come, because they have changed their basic identity. But may I suggest that we not be overly concerned at the moment with ultimate corporate power and its many manifestations.

Nor do I propose to consider here the small, day-to-day pragmatic administrative decision, even though it has a way of sometimes precipitating circumstances of striking proportion. I mention these small daily decisions only because those on the receiving end of the smallest of such equate them with power, and they are right.

The sort of power about which I would remind us, and the whole point of this discussion, is the potential power, sometimes undiscovered or dormant, of the bonding that comes with responsibility; of the unmistakable man-thing link between the chief executive and the physical institution; and the man-persons link between the chief executive and the people who are the true institution. If one can agree with the previously postulated *pathway principle,* then it can naturally follow that it is the *pathway* which couples the individual and the institution. It is the *journey* which binds them together and from which they may draw mutual power. No person other than the chief administrator can make this power connection. No one else associated with, employed by, or in attendance at the institution can feel exactly this power-bond-opportunity.

The story of any school, college, or university has always been, to a large degree, the combined stories of those who have been called to positions of top leadership. For the most part, they have been stories of adventure. In good times the journey has been characterized by exhilaration and by promise; in more unfortunate times it has been filled with frustration and disappointment. But it has never been dull. However imperfect the men, however clumsy the institutions, however meandering the course, the indestructible academic organism has moved ahead. The pathway *has* led to somewhere. Tomorrow, history can tell us where. Today, men and institutions cannot.

II. Problems, Problems

THE POINT does not have to be made that problems are inherent in the living of life, in the management of human affairs, and in the ongoing stream of institutional existence. Problems are necessary for progress and, as such, are significantly important to the person who exercises final authority in their solution. Indeed, without the presence of problems one could make a case that there would be no need for authority, no need for decision, no need for leadership. And yet, many of us behave as if we could accomplish so much more if only we could diminish the time and energy spent in "problem areas." The truth of the matter is that students and faculties and boards could do very well without us if our institutions were to become the problem-free, intellectually independent communities of which we dream. The receiving, the consideration, and solving of problems is the major expender of presidential or principalian energy. Abdication of this primary responsibility should indicate that we have delegated away our charge to deal with daily and long-term difficulty. Or, that rather than to attempt to solve problems, we are spending an inordinate amount of time at the futile exercise of assuring ourselves and our constituencies that neither we nor our institution has any.

100 Problems 100

Above the door to the office of the chief administrator there should perhaps be a theater-type marquee, done in academic taste and subtlety of course, reflecting the words "100 Problems 100 (count 'em); appearing daily 9 to 5; matinee performances on Saturdays and Sundays with special showings at any hour without special arrangement."

A nice added touch would be an accompanying bill proclaiming, "Through these portals pass the most beautiful problems in the world!"

Any why not? In good times and poor, in institutional sickness and in health, for better or for worse—we, the institution we serve, and the profession to which we have dedicated our lives are a somewhat fragile yet never-ending union, a union tied together by the need for continuous and mutual replenishment of confidence, the reassurance of relationship, and the redeclaration of common purpose. Any chief executive who ignores or modifies the responsibility for his part of the bargain has made a bad contract.

Problem solving is a practicing art as surely as working with one's head and heart and hands in oil, water color, tempera, acrylics, wood, metal, or clay. And it can give the practicing "artist" as much satisfaction in accomplishment. To carry the analogy much further would find one quickly in over his head, but many of us can be justifiably proud of a series of one-man shows that neither the general public nor the majority of the inside constituency will ever see. The disappointments and the achievements of the solitary problem solver are to be kept to himself, and part of the "art" is the suppression of a sometimes overwhelming desire to share details with close colleagues in order to garner approval, praise, or sympathy. The responsibility to respect the points of view and keep the confidences of discussants and confrontants when one is in the role of referee and jurist is essential to the practice of the art. Just who judges the artist or the art work or the critic are questions which, mercifully, need not be answered here. But I suspect that, as is the usual case with the true artist, one is usually most critical of his own work. And, through such criticism, he can improve upon the result of his next endeavor.

Who Needs Problems?

Any human enterprise which proposes to advance requires problems. Since none of us would wish to admit, I suspect, that he is standing still, then the presence of problems becomes a necessity. This would seem to be, at first glance, a massive piece of rationalization: problems are perennial; nothing can be done to do away with problems permanently; therefore, we are better off to tolerate them and, perhaps, even learn to live with them. But our consideration must go beyond this attitude of reluctant resignation because the forward movement of any idea, any concept, any proposal, any positive future possibility is directly related to the satisfactory solving of specific problems which will inevitably stand in the way. Often problems and solutions can be anticipated and the theorists will come surprisingly close to their forecasts. More often, an idea launched out of a nonscientific combination of a visceral feeling and a working faith winds its way through problem after problem, becoming ever stronger for doing so. Who is it that makes the decision, at each head-on problem collision, whether or not the idea is bigger than the problem and thus deserves another chance? The president or the principal or the superintendent makes the decision, acting upon the best accumulation of advice and counsel he can muster from all sources available to him.

Much has been written of the "style" of persons in authority and of the importance of style in dealing with problem areas within their spheres of authority. If we can return to the concept of administrative problem solving as an art (as opposed to a "science"), then the need for a blend of creativity and style in the artist can make its own point. Creativity and style are singularly personal. If they are major factors in the critical decisions of problem solving, then the necessarily unilateral and seemingly arbitrary decisions should be accompanied by two additional elements: objectivity and compassion. Again, we are describing two essential characteristics of the artist.

Who needs problems? If one takes upon himself the responsibility to lead creatively and objectively and compassionately, his own style can be effective only insofar as these personal characteristics ring true and only if there are problems that should be solved. It would appear that the problems relating to our realm of Academia will always be in a greater abundance than the effective problem solvers, so the future for highly qualified and high quality educational administrators seems safe enough.

The Trouble with Trouble

At least three traits make trouble an uncomfortable and negative experience : it gives little or no warning ; it comes in bunches ; and it increases geometrically in a devastatingly short period of time. Fortunately, however, there can be corresponding positive traits in the person of an effective administrator: flexibility, consistency, and strength. The trouble with trouble is that it often causes a series of negative reactions which compound themselves as the process of overcoming the difficulty reaches full force. When we apply this compounding process to the goings-on in Academia we see still further complication, because the very nature of educational institutions dictates that their inhabitants ask questions. Asking questions can be dangerous : it can lead from trouble to big trouble. That is, it can lead to a temporary (or permanent) period of total negative effect upon an institution and its people. Whether or not that negative period can be ridden out, turned around, and transformed into a permanent and positive institutional stance and to positive personal attitudes depends upon top leadership. It depends in great measure upon the chief executive's flexibility, his consistency, and his strength. Another way to express this is to counter the potentially negative aspects of trouble by remaining . . . *Cool!* Trouble starts with "T," which rhymes with "C," which stands for "Cool"—with apologies to Professor Harold Hill, Meredith Willson's *Music Man.* If the reader wishes to pursue this further, he can develop his own analogy, although the idea of countering the distressing atmosphere of a billiard parlor with the excitement of a big, brass band is not too bad, at that.

The trouble with trouble is that we are not ready, in most cases, to see its positive possibilities. The chief administrator cannot escape his responsibility to do just that. If trouble quickly multiplies, the feeling of helplessness to do anything about it can multiply at an even greater rate. The shameful position of accepting defeat by default is then dangerously near unless the man or woman in final authority is dedicated to the idea that there are positive possibilities in any problem situation and unless he or she can muster support from colleagues who can turn the mule around and convince him to begin to plow a positive furrow. Unfortunately, and as we have learned from a recurring story out of regional folklore, it sometimes takes the appropriate application of a club the size of a 2x4 to get his attention before he can be convinced.

The Rise and Fall of a Problem

Out of the nebulous swirl of institutional activity, a potential problem is spun off into an environment which can, if optimum negative conditions prevail, grow from a single cell, normal or mutated, into a monster. Monstrous problems, like monsters themselves, are seldom born full-grown. The development of the problem threat, whether it follows a normal growth pattern or a superaccelerated rate, must be followed closely by the person who has the ultimate responsibility for its destruction or capture. Let us suppose that the first faint shudder of the stirrings for curricular revolt are not perceived by the president or the principal. A chain of events begins to unfold which can eventually involve every segment of the institution and can place the chief executive in the unfortunate position of dealing with a problem rather than with an idea. He can quickly find himself on the outside looking in. He can find himself wishing to support what he feels is the need for reform but not in possession of necessary facts and feelings concerning the pros and cons of early discussion. Not being an active participant *from the beginning,* he is lost in the problems of arbitration of an argument rather than in the exhilarating exercise of the joint development of an idea. He may even be forced to kill the idea in order to keep the peace.

Previously, we inferred that "monster" had a negative connotation. Indeed such are born and begin to grow and must be stepped on. But the harnessing of a monster of another sort—an energy-charged idea of great promise—can be a major contribution to a complacent, peaceful-for-the-wrong-reasons school or college. We must beware the monster, but never write him off as a totally destructive force. We must be aware of his hatching and his early incubation in order to assist in his rearing if it is determined to allow him to grow to maturity. Again, one might think of it in terms of being in the positive position of supporting or discouraging an idea rather than in the negative position of getting rid of a problem.

Back to (Normal)

Unless one defines terms, he is likely to conclude that there is no such thing as normal and, following, that to discuss prospects for getting "back to normal" is an exercise for campaigning politicians and optimistic economists. Normality, we tend to believe, exists only momentarily, if at all—especially if we try to pin it down to the everyday operation of an enterprise as structurally complex and as emotionally volatile as an educational institution. The believability of spending a day in normalcy is equated only with the questionable advantage of calling in sick and spending the day in bed. We have not yet defined "normal." In the academic kingdom and, particularly, in regard to positions of high authority, normal can only be a synonym for chaos. Those in such authoritarian positions and those who aspire to such positions must realize that it is not enough to tolerate chaos; one must actually *enjoy* it in order to be completely effective. At best, academic chaos is an everchanging sort with opportunities for ordered leadership coming from an overview of the entire spectrum rather than overconcentration upon one narrow band or another. These opportunities are all too rare in reality and testify to the absolute necessity for periodic time-perspective exercises by top leadership. He who sees the total rainbow can best determine the relationships of the reds to the violets. In our system, only the person in whom final authority is vested has the potential vantage point for such an overview. The fact that he is not afforded the opportunity to step back regularly for a wide-angle look at his institution, thus more clearly seeing its prospects and its pathways, is more than unfortunate for the continuing health of both school and individual. If time for such periodic survey were to be built into the machinery, then a return to the normalcy of chaos could carry a new dimension. New energy and new insights could be added to the enjoyment of problem solving.

Problems and Promises

For every problem there seems to be what we might call an internal and an external promise. The *internal* promise can be considered to be related to the problem itself. It can assume, oftentimes falsely, that "things will work themselves out" or that "every cloud has a silver lining." The *external* promise surmises a sort of guarantee by the person in charge that a solution will be found. On the surface it would appear that these two promises are apples and oranges and cannot, therefore, be compared in the traditional manner of the mathematician. A closer examination might reveal that they are not so very different and that the one sometimes needs the other if progress toward effective solution is to be realized.

Both the internal and external promises of a problem are singularly related: the internal promise is related to the problem itself, the external promise to the solver. Both are tied to a time sequence. The administrative leader can use either or both as he moves toward a decision which will solve the problem in a way which is best for the majority. If he is not convinced that each problem facing his institution is in some manner solvable and if he is not convinced that he alone is responsible for the final decision following an accumulation of evidence, recommendations, suggestions, and time and weighing of all known alternatives, then he cannot lead. He can "front" for his school or college. He can sit in the chair and govern by the book. But he cannot lead.

In an increasing number of situations, time has seemingly become an unaffordable luxury in the management of the affairs of Academia. Time to consult; time to ponder; time to gather an abundance of opinion; time to decide. These traditional characteristics of the academic administrative process are said to be in progressively short supply. Anxious faculty and impatient students would group them together in a category of "time to stall." Indeed, when one is facing a crisis of revolutionary proportion, he must summon, quickly and from within himself, the strength and wisdom necessary for almost instant decisions. Sometimes these decisions solve the problem; sometimes they do not. There is no time for reflection and, if one is lucky, he can exert positive leadership through force of personality and persuasion. But in the main, we have been guilty of abandoning the trust which boards have placed in us and the trust which our constituencies expect of us. We have too often convinced ourselves (or let ourselves be convinced) that we do not have time to consider the most essential elements of problem solving: the intrinsic promises of the problems themselves; the promise of self-confidence that we can move the institution positively, if most times ponderously, toward solution—toward solution that lasts longer than tomorrow or next week.

III. Making Things Happen

IDEAS ARE THE BASIC INGREDIENTS of which innovative programs are made. The program potential seems to get better with seasoning and spicing, and with stirring. Like some ancient recipe for witch's brew or some medieval alchemist's formulae, the more and varied the ideas stirred into the cauldron, the more interesting becomes the resulting mixture. A pinch of this and a dash of that, often added most unscientifically, provide the flavor and the excitement necessary to turn a bundle of stray ideas into a new and appealing educational adventure.

Eye of newt and tongue of frog can take on a very respectable role in the preparation of Academian pottage and that most ridiculed of social enigmas, the committee, appropriately assumes its rightful place around the edge of the crucible. The magic of the transformation of separate and dissimilar idea segments into a homogeneous and totally new substance is as amazing as the process which can bring it about. Development of this sort requires a team effort; the original "Double, double toil and trouble" was chanted in three-part harmony. The Team is a cumbersome and sometimes quarrelsome phenomenon which usually moves with the speed yet the eventual effectiveness of a glacier. The team process cannot, or should not, be hurried, for although the participants are not always sure just how the product will turn out or just what the ingredients will be, they are certain that time should be the unquestioned constant. A president or a principal in too much of a hurry to taste the broth not only runs the risk of losing a potentially fine new program, he can also strangle team initiative and place himself in a most precarious personal position with his magicians. And who wants to be turned into a toad? A prince, maybe, but the remote possibility is not worth the risk.

25

The Team Man

Out of necessity, or because of his or her own personal preference, many educational administrators in top authority rely heavily on a team of high echelon colleagues for counsel and for direction of specific areas within the institution. It helps to keep the peace during "administrative council" meetings if the members of the team are of reasonably compatible personality and their number is reasonably small. It helps the team process and the end product of their deliberations if they are seldom in complete agreement yet are endowed with an abundance of experience and intuition, a sixth sense, and a feeling for the total institution. Whether a chief executive inherits a team or, more rarely, is able to build his own, he will hopefully find most of these plus factors in the makeup of the team and *will make use of them*. A group of strong individuals should be expected to have strong and diverse opinions and thus to have some difficulty in arriving at a consensus. The members of such a group also expect to be, and deserve to be, led by a strong person. This concept is not as contradictory as one might think. An administrative team can have its greatest moments of frustration when it arrives at the obvious point in deliberation when further discussion becomes useless vocal exercise. The president, or his counterpart, must then pull the loose strands together, cut and tie the ragged edges, bind the ends, sweep out the shop, and move the team along to the next consideration.

The foregoing proposition assumes, of course, that the president meets with the team, that it is his council or coun*sel*. This is not always the president's choice, but it would seem to be essential for at least two reasons : any eventual presidential decision is more apt to be more equitable (though no more easy) when as many facts and as much reaction to such facts are available to the final decision maker at *first hand;* and the members of the team are more likely to feel a partnership in policy making rather than a quasi-attachment to a disoriented, predecision series of sublevel caucuses. The chief executive must not only be a working member of the team. He must assume active leadership. There is a fine and fragile line between the granting of full partnership for team discussion and recommendation and the denial of voting in a final decision. *Collective opinion* in the counseling and advising of the president is as near as an administrative team should come to policy decision. We have come once again to view executive leadership as a practicing art. And to suggest that the chief administrator who calls himself a "team man" must, after all, finally stand alone.

Team Consensus vs. *Team Responsibility*

The team approach to educational problem solving must be dependent upon the personality, character, and wishes of the chief executive. The team must be *his* team and its members must be willing to be used as *he* will use them. They must give him their loyalties (including, on occasion, their loyal opposition), their talents, and their intimate knowledge of each specific area and institutional constituency represented. They must do this because he assumes singular responsibility for any consensus. "The administration," that nameless, faceless target for occasional student wrath, public anger, and faculty grumbling is so much mist and cobweb. But the president has a name, the principal has a face, and the chairman of the school board has a telephone number, and none of them is unlisted.

Sooner or later, the question of accountability comes up, and the ensuing encounter is a personal one. No committee is capable of a person-to-person attempt to resolve a misunderstanding or to explain a one-man decision. Traditionally, none but the foolhardy or the disturbed issued the challenge, "Let's me and all of you fight," and, though this is happening more frequently within recent years, it always ends as "no contest," because a committee or a team does not and should not put its title on the line.

Administrative team democracy, in the general sense of the term, is participatory rather than decisional. A chief executive cannot grant a portion of his responsibility or power to others, no matter if they are the most diligent, most enlightened, most intelligent individuals in all of Academia. Consensus among keen and compassionate minds and hearts is one thing; ultimate decision by group vote is quite another. Sifting ideas leading to new programs, hammering out projected policies, taking inventory of institutional strengths and weaknesses are all tasks for a combined effort by valued members of a dedicated and thoughtful team, but the decision to "make things happen" is singularly that of the chief administrator. He should be hired, then retained or dismissed primarily on the basis of his ability to accumulate the pros and cons of questions and problems basic to the life and health of the institution and its people and on his strength and courage to then make decisions.

At the Point of Action

The precise point at which the combination of a wide variety of forces and the dictates of time requires action is difficult to discern and even more difficult to define. *The* point, I am sure, is no more than momentary. Yet the seemingly endless and frustrating yet exciting period of search before the point of action and the sometimes lingering feelings of doubt and misgiving in the aftermath can cover an appreciable amount of time. We should probably therefore call it a *process* of action and not a *point* of action, though the latter remains the critical instant which will set the new vehicle in motion, send it back to the drawing board, or put it on the shelf. Once again, we find the predominant element to be one of unique character or style, and we find that the overwhelming institutional responsibility delegated by charter or board to one person cannot be shared.

Whether or not the contemplative decision maker exhibits an outward casual appearance or one of deep agony really matters little to the eventual decision or to the programs affected by it. It might matter a great deal to the *people* around him, even though his feelings and his manner of expressing or reflecting them are his. Experience and observation seem to indicate that differences in executive personality and style are recognized and understood by constituent groups and that while everyone expects a decision, few expect an explanation and even fewer demand one. This may or may not be good, and attitudes are changing in this regard. The future will almost certainly add a new dimension to the process and point of action. How much of the process leading to the decision should be shared with how many is a perpetual question. I leave it to the men and women who must answer it for themselves.

It is rather paradoxical that a periodic resurgence of a mass sense of social urgency pushes us toward quicker decisions, yet the very problems demanding processes and points of action are of such magnitude that we should be taking longer to answer them. Perhaps the technique of the Western gunfighter will fill the vacuum unless we *make time*. He would have us shoot from the hip, hope we hit the target for which we were hired, then disappear slowly and unchallenged into the sunset and relative anonymity until another job requires that sort of "attention." Surely, we are strong enough to prevent this from happening. Surely, we can still choose our time and place and point of action, and though the result can never please everyone who comes within its sphere of influence, it can be as equitable, as understandable, and as bloodless as possible, given the chance of human error in the process and the acceptance of human fallibility in the action taken.

One Desk, One Chair, One Man

The desk and *the* chair bespeak authority. There is only one such desk and one such chair per institution. Only one man or one woman sits behind *the desk* and in *the chair,* during office hours, at any rate, and when the desk top is clear and the chair is empty the institution feels the difference. In a less complex day, long gone, college and university presidents could be away for lengthy periods of time raising money, recruiting faculty, making speeches, and lobbying in the state capitol; it was business as usual for the institution. These were necessary presidential separations, and the many questions and concerns with which he ordinarily dealt simply waited for his return. The general pace was slower; students and faculty and boards were a great deal less inclined toward impatience. This helped to permit an accumulation of postponed decisions which, when desk and chair again welcomed their accustomed occupant, were usually handled unilaterally and with dispatch. Simpler days, but not with simple problems. *The old man* worked longer hours and could seldom exer-

cise the practice of delegation; he could not afford to hire anyone to
whom to delegate. We should stop to consider, more often than we
do, how our administrative predecessors survived those years. They
were either resigned to or thrived upon the work load (journals and
diaries overwhelmingly reveal the latter) and taught classes, erased
blackboards, and stoked furnaces in addition to their administrative
duties. Moreover, they often held their positions for thirty, forty, or
more years.

It would be unrealistic and unfair to imply that today's president
or principal is heartbeat and brain wave of a school or college. We
know that the *faculty* is the college, that the *students* are the reason
for the college to exist, and that the *governing board* is responsible
for fiscal responsibility and highest level policy. We should also recognize that the covey, flock, gaggle, herd, or colony of administrators
(upon reflection, "pride" seems a better descriptive term for a couple
of reasons) exists only as a group of supportive specialists who serve
the central teaching and learning process. Historically, the chief executive was a member of the faculty, but, alas, he was metamorphosed
into an "administrator" and had to be satisfied to take his institutional
stature as a member of the herd. Unique and in power to be sure, but
irrevocably an administrator.

It would also be unfair, and untrue, to intimate that nothing begins
to happen without the principal's presence or without the superintendent's knowledge. Ideas and germs of ideas usually start where
the teacher meets the student. But a request or a demand for implementation comes, at last, to *the desk, the chair,* and *the man.*

Constituent Expectations

The interactional highways between constituents and chief administrator are of many levels and appropriately carry traffic in several
directions. And yet, reduced to simplest terms, there must be a simple
wagon-track road of trust. Educational constituencies include those
familiar categories inside the institution, those valued and varied
alliance groups "outside" the organizational structure, and the great,
gray public beyond—some interested, some indifferent, some hostile,

and most not bothering consciously to determine why. The charting of interactions among these constituencies would make a fascinating series of diagrams. Then, considered separately here, there is the administrator-in-charge. What does each of the aforementioned constituent groups, both internal and external, expect of him or of her? In a question far less frequently asked, what does he or she expect of them? Rather than to painstakingly delineate specific relationships, some of which we have already considered in part and which would require a parallel listing of traits and attitudes which can change or modify within considered groups and individuals, let's paint with a broad brush. A single, wide and heavy stroke in each direction should be labeled "trust."

If basic trust is violated on the part of either a constituency or the chief executive—or, if damaged, is not quickly and mutually repaired —the relationship is in serious jeopardy. A manifestation of distrust, in either direction or in both, can then affect the total school or college and begin to erode the institutional confidence of those who work within it and on its behalf. What should each constituency ask from the person who heads the university or the elementary school? Trust. What should he expect from them? Trust. A mutual confidence can withstand the buffetings of unrest, criticism, rumor, gossip, fear, and other types of poisoned darts which can tear relationships apart and can render an institution all but lifeless.

An Executive Executes!

Several years ago while in the process of selling a piece of real property, I received in due course some papers and a covering letter from the escrow officer. The letter said, in part, "Enclosed are a deed and a termite inspection authorization. Please have your wife executed and return at once." It was not specified whether *I* was to return or was merely expected to send the body. Having neither the desire nor the authority to order the execution of my wife (I felt somewhat differently about the real estate agent) I could only assume that the escrow officer had inadvertently hit an extra key on the typewriter and really meant to have my wife execute the documents so that the exterminator could be asked to execute the termites, if such were discovered. One thing was certain, an execution was expected and, further, I was in an inescapable position to see to it. For those who like to know how things turn out, my wife executed the documents, the exterminator spent three days discovering that there were no termites, and the escrow officer ran away with the real estate agent.

There is no escape for the person in final authority from decision, from action, from execution, from making things happen. An executive executes. It is true that with an elapse of time, a postponed decision sometimes eliminates the reason to make it. It is also true that *most* times it grows from a small and relatively simple decision to a large and complex one. There are times when taking no action is an action in itself, but these times should be relatively rare and should involve the previously described deliberative process leading rationally to the point of no action required. The important corollary here, it would seem, is that the person or the constituency asking for a decision be told, in all but special confidential cases, why the "no-action" route was followed. And please, not in the form of a memo. Memos have, I would venture, broken down more communication than they have helped. For my colleagues in institutions of more than 2,500 students and 200 faculty members, I hereby recognize that face-to-face explanations are not always possible. But surely, a personal note requiring the same number of words and reflecting a certain warmth and request for understanding is better than the chilly and intrinsically ominous memo.

The Wizard of If

We have concluded that the total process of making things happen is most often a long and tedious exercise involving the ideas of many and the refinements of many more. I have suggested that the chief administrator be a part of that process as time, energy, and institutional priorities permit and that the greater his participation the better equipped he will be to render a decision at the point of action. Deliberation is a necessity, but the instant of moving ahead or staying behind will come and, after it comes, the result must be lived with.

The basic responsibility to defend not only the decision, which is his, but the program, which has been jointly developed, lies with the only employed professional who can speak for the total enterprise. Interestingly enough, if the program is a success, it is *their* success and if not it becomes *his* folly. This fact of institutional life should not be bothersome to the chief executive. He did not seek the position in order to exhalt his personal position in Academia or in the community; he did not accept it expecting universal praise or popularity. When the history of the institution is written or updated, the author will quite properly chronicle the events, both meritorious and unfortunate, which occurred during Mr., Mrs., Miss, or Ms. So-and so's administration. So very much of each depends upon the forces which act upon the person and his time; so much depends upon the performance of those around him; so much depends upon *if*.

So the man or woman of authority at all levels of American education, private or public; the stirrer of faculty promise and, indirectly, of student performance; the decision maker, the defender of the troops and of the strategy and of the outcome of the battle, becomes, as time will tell and as history will record, *The Wizard of If*.

IV. Listen!

HOLD IT UP TO YOUR EAR and you can hear the ocean."
Listening to the soft murmur of the conch shell is symbolic of a phenomenon which began for most of us in childhood and which remains with most of us throughout our lives. Whether the actual setting was the seashore or grandmother's parlor, we actually heard the ocean, even though rationality or instant comparison told us otherwise. The peculiar movement of air current between the deep recesses of inner shell and middle ear produced a sound which, with strong suggestion and an even stronger will, became at once the seven seas. We closed our eyes, held our breaths, plugged up the other ear with a finger, and listened to the surf as it pounded on an undiscovered shore in a beckoning and faraway land. On location, with sand between our toes and sea spray in our nostrils, the believability could perhaps be understood. But on a dark December afternoon in Nebraska, with every sense straining its mooring lines, we not only heard the ocean—we smelled the tar and oakum, tasted the salt crusted on our lips, and felt a ten-knot sea breeze that whipped against our bare legs and tousled our hair. How often do we still hear what we want to hear, hear what others tell us we will hear if we listen carefully enough, believe what we are hearing because it is the easiest thing to believe under the circumstances?

A chief administrator spends a great deal of his time listening. He is the unique listener of the institution. He cannot really listen without unstopping that other ear. He must make a deeply conscious effort to screen out some of the siren sounds of the Pacific or the Atlantic, but he must also retain his sense of adventure to the extent that steering a course between and beyond Charybdis and Scylla is still the challenge of the conch shell. He must listen more attentively and more actively than any other individual within his school or college. To him, more than to anyone else, listening is an *active* art.

It demands concentration, the ability to distill mixtures into essences while discussion is under way, and a mind which can search out alternate routes while the discussion is pursuing a single one. Above all, it demands discovery of the critical difference between hearing and listening, together with constantly reminding oneself of that difference.

Attitudinal Listening

Perhaps more than anything else listening is an attitude. The conversation may be casual or on a subject which can have great influence upon the institution, but the attitude of the listener (on both sides of the conversation) makes the critical difference in communication.

NEGATIVE listening, under my definition of the term, reflects a preconceived conclusion, not only toward conversational content but also toward outcome. Two negative listeners are wasting a good deal of what ought to be valuable time. Because regardless of the worth of the words that are flying back and forth across the room, they are unheard and unheeded—a collection of laryngeal contractions and air vibrations that stop short of either cerebral register or understanding. The negative listener predecides, and predecision is not exactly a desirable characteristic of leadership. Many a new idea or possible worthwhile change in direction can be choked off, perhaps forever discarded, because the chief administrator is engaged in non-listening and predecision. "We don't have the money; it didn't work when we tried it five years ago; the faculty would never vote it through; the trustees are too conservative to even give it consideration." These can be verbalized responses of negative listening, caused by the very first exploratory sentences of a presentation or proposal. Even worse, their proponents can be turned off while the scheduling of an appointment for their discussion is being attempted. Negative listening, determined by negative attitudes, can only result in negative conclusions. Many times such negative conclusions result in the weakening or nonstrengthening of the institution. Responsibility of that magnitude demands more than a negative ear.

NEUTRAL listening, again my definition, goes beyond the guarantee of an open mind. "Open mind" almost says, "Show me!" This attitude, or the interpretation that this is the attitude, can also cause an auditory nerve blockage between ear and brain. The projected attitude of neutral listening can just as easily take the form of "Let's look at the possibilities." It assures that the channel is clear for both listening *and* speaking. It says, I think, that principal or superintendent has made time and *atmosphere* available for objective listening and for what can hopefully lead to a rewarding conversation about a problem, a project, or a point of difference. It says that the president or chancellor or board chairman has welcomed an interview which places no phony barriers in the way of effective communication. Neutral listening cannot guarantee complete mutual agreement but it does much to establish a base of mutual trust. And, even if the ultimate answer must be in the negative or the idea must be discarded, the personal bond between listeners can be stronger than before. A neutral listener can influence the give-and-take of discussion by keeping the brain channel open when it is his turn to *listen*. The responsibility of the chief executive is uniquely important because, once again, he or she must be the chief listener.

Who, then, is a POSITIVE listener? One who uses both "ears"— the ear of the adventurer and the ear of practicality—one who is charmed by the promises of the conch shell but who also searches for ways to test the practical potentialities of promises and then for ways to make the promises come true. The positive listener should be the most active of all because, assuming that it is agreed that an idea holds promise, he must punctuate his listening with "We will find a way to do it." He has gone a step further than neutral: He becomes an active participant in the first phase of growth toward accomplishment, and all because he listened positively. Most times when people in education listen positively they begin to speak and to act positively. Too theoretical or too idealistic, you say? May be you were not listening positively.

No One to Listen To

The keeping of confidences at the highest level must be among the most carefully guarded responsibilities of any educational chief administrator. The invitation to "come into the office and I'll be pleased to listen" can turn into an unhealing wound if the request (stated or implied) for confidential treatment is broken by the listener. Many times the need for an objective listener is sought by various persons or groups within an institution or by members of an interested and potentially supportive public. The president's office, for example, should be among the few places on a campus where certain personal and institutional feelings, opinions, doubts, fears, and concerns can be privately discussed. With the knowledge that the chief listener is a respecter of confidence, the invitation can always be accepted. One small breach, or two, or several and the listener soon has no one to listen to. On most occasions, the confidential subject under discussion will involve colleagues or specific programs or situations which reflect upon the behavior or the judgment of colleagues. Let the listener beware or at least be prepared to assume conversational control at the appropriate point. Whether or not direct action or discreet inquiry is called for ought to be determined very quickly if an astute listener exercises just a minimal amount of probing. Gossip, in the guise of helpful sharing of confidential information, can usually be identified in short order. Once again we see listening as an active art rather than as a passive occupation. To be other than an active listener in matters of a confidential nature is to be reduced to a Lilliputian level of leadership.

The reverse side of the chief executive's keeping of shared confidences involves the repeating of careless presidential or principalian talk by the other party. Again, let the chief beware. Sometimes, even after one has listened with calm and understanding, the temptation to think out loud immediately or to share in the instant pondering of "whys" and "ifs" becomes too great. The listener has then surrendered *his* right to confidence. The balance of responsibility between the chief executive and others in this situation must be weighted in the direction of the chief executive, and it should be recognized and respected by him or by her. *Anything* the top man or woman says is repeatable, not because it was particularly profound or enlightening, but because he or she said it. Their words are public property. And, though pontification is inherent in the Papacy, many a chief administrator has succumbed to self-elevation to the Most High. Any segment of power should be used with a combination of caution and compassion—for the sake of others, and realistically for the sake of one's self.

What Big Ears You Have!

Sometimes, if you listen very carefully, you can hear yourself. This might be a sort of fifth-and-a-half sense and ought to be industriously developed because some of the things you say to yourself just might be superior to some of the things that are being said around you. Anatomically, we cannot explain the phenomenon of self-listening. There is no room in the middle ear for another bone or membrane, nor in the auditory nerve cable for another strand of wire. But however difficult it may be to describe the process, one should cultivate the habit of talking to himself and, in turn, of paying heed as he listens. That uncomfortable and gnawing feeling that in spite of all rational advice and of all valid evidence you should take a completely different tack does not come out of nowhere. It comes directly through that auditory bypass, from small voice to big ear to pit of stomach.

We have talked about the responsibility of the chief administrator to listen. We have been guilty of thinking most about that responsibility in terms of faculty and administrative colleagues and of the public. Students have been described as the "forgotten center" of the educational universe and, though I suspect there is some degree of truth in this allegation, no modern-day administrator can say that he or she is not spending an ever greater percentage of "listening time" with students. The bigger one's ears, the greater the chance to listen and then to achieve understanding.

Perhaps we ought to think more about the levels of listening and, in so doing, consider that there is no easily reached *level of communication*. The commonly understood link is the desire for a better educational environment. But it is not encased in common verbiage. When students and the president or students and the principal involve themselves in discussion, they have, quite appropriately, their own ways of self-expression and their own ways of listening and their own ideas on how to reach the same objective. The only tools they have are words—the language—and the interpretation of generation-separated language requires a healthy attitude toward listening. Here, one has to give points to the young people, for they more often say what they mean. Some administrators to whom they present their views have a bothersome habit of waiting to talk rather than listening and, when they do speak, of using the curiously obscuring rhetoric of Academia.

No responsible student expects instantaneous acceptance of his suggestions (nor an irresponsible student of his demands) but he has every right to expect an active listener and an honest, clearly stated response. This should be especially true when the student is in conversation with the only man or woman who can listen and respond with authority. It is no accident, I think, that persons with the biggest ears make the biggest decisions.

I Listen, You Listen, He or She Listens;
We Listen, You Listen, They Listen

In the process of *group dynamics,* to reach back a few years for a comfortable phrase, the recorded verbal interaction was charted. Today, we have *encounter groups* and *sensitivity sessions,* whose verbal or tactile manifestations are also recorded through techniques of diagraming. Lines and arrows still reveal the active relationships between individuals or knots of individuals within a group. And the primary river of intercommunication must still be strings of words. The cathartic or psychotherapeutic values of such encounters notwithstanding, the game is still communication. As a matter of fact, the charting of interaction as it occurs within an ordinary committee meeting would make most interesting patterns. I hope we have not reached the point of allowing faculty meeetings to become tactile (either out of violence or in a search for love), but the endless flow

of words, the solid and dotted lines drawn between the stars and supporting actors, the revealing of deep human emotions are all present.
And who is listening?

What about the seemingly passive participation of the total listener? Can he be an active listener and a passive participant? I
would suggest that lines can be drawn between listeners and listeners
if the recorder is astute enough to do so and that such "lines of silence" have much to do with the intricacies of group communication
and with the success of the work which groups set for themselves.

Complete conjugation of the verb "to listen" involves all personal
pronouns. The practice of effective group communication should
involve equally proportioned amounts of listening by all persons in
the group. In theory, we can clearly see the familiar diagrams and
can hope to widen the picture to include both verbal and silent lines
of intercommunication. In reality, it is not any more likely that we
will have total *listening* participation than total *verbal* participation.
But one thing seems clear: The listening process is infectious. Just
as one "catches" malaria, one can catch active listening. The chief
executive, I venture to suggest, should then be in the role of a gently
subtle mosquito whose bite may finally prove to be neither gentle or
subtle. He is then working to create, rather than to prevent, an epi-
demic. The faster it spreads the better for all concerned. We can only
feel sorry that those who are naturally or conditionally immune will
never enjoy the chills and fever of full-scale active listening.

Sticks and Stones and Ears

Once in a while the chief executive opens his ears and hears personal criticism. Though he is still semi-isolated because of the location
of his office and semi-insulated because of the vestigial respect for
his "office," the criticisms filter through. They are now beginning to
come on a direct line from any and every corner of the campus and
the community. Personal criticism is many times deserved, even
earned, but it is no easier to take. Great opportunities for rationalization present themselves and, I think, more often than most of us
would care to admit, are seized upon with relish: "Nobody's perfect;

they're only jealous of the position and the power; I can't possibly please everyone; they don't realize the strain I'm under." As temporarily comforting as these cliché-wrapped reactions may be, the facts are that once personal criticism has been discovered, it hurts, and that whatever rationale one uses to feel better he cannot completely shut his ears or his conscience to the possibility that the criticism might well be founded in truth.

When one in authority hears personal criticism, there is often a very human and immediate reaction: the temptation to somehow spread the blame or to widen the sphere of responsibility and thus reduce his own personal responsibility. Indeed, others may have been in on the action which resulted in the criticism. But the one personification of the institution is the chief administrator, and when scornful fingers are pointed, it is almost impossible to point at more than one person at a time. "The Administration" is, finally, the person in charge. Like it or not, the principal or the president is not, and should not be immune from personal criticism any more than any other member of the professional staff. It is inherent in the position that *blame,* justified or not, is finally vested in the chief. Sticks and stones have broken bones and words have, too, when those in authority have refused to accept personally the responsibility for institutional mistakes. Words, like sticks and stones, will always hurt. There ought not to be any sort of sensitivity screen which filters out personal hurts; they are as much a part of the job as personal triumphs. Messages *should* get through, even those which may bring bad news or personal pain.

Listening Is a Beginning

Listening is the point at which understanding, reconciliation, moving ahead with an idea—indeed, progress of any sort—begins. A gesture, an apology, or an idea can be verbalized for as long as vocal cords respond to brain waves. But until someone listens, there has been no beginning of the process which brings people together. We forget this more often than we remember it and are thus frustrated or disappointed or angry because nothing happens. Of course, *some-*

thing happens: Usually the potential for progress suffers a net loss. And deficit positions in human relations are just as difficult to overcome as deficit positions in the budget, and they are likely to last longer.

A man or woman who has been appointed to the top administrative position in schools, colleges, and universities must be active at both ends of the discussion and as both listener and verbal participant. As we speak, we are too often unaware of shadings which our listeners give to what seem to us to be clearly black or white comments. As we listen, we are too often insensitive to the spoken subtleties and nuances of those attempting to communicate with us. Agreement needs at least two persons who are both aware and sensitive and who can actively listen and speak. With requirements such as these, the wonder of the process is that it happens at all. The magic that makes it happen is that someone takes the first step, and it is the positive listener who most often puts his ear forward first.

Resolving personal differences, including those involving the chief executive himself, puts listening to its greatest test. Emotion plays its loudest strains in such situations, and listening can become a near impossibility. One hand must be extended first. The active listener ought to be more easily able to control emotion and thus in a better position to extend that hand. If this is true, then the administrator in final authority carries the "first listening" responsibility and should be able to effect the beginning which is sought from both sides of the fence. A fence which needlessly stands in the way of advancement toward a mutually acceptable common ground, a ground which should stand above conflict and which is a credit to the institution and all of its people.

Listen!

V. Decisions Aren't Forever

BACKING UP AND STARTING OVER need not reflect a poor administrator, only a poor decision. The eventual and perhaps permanent effect upon any educational institution can be more positive with a half-dozen admitted mistakes than with the blind reenforcement of one unfortunate decision; a decision which, for a possible variety of reasons, may have lost its original validity or which was simply wrong at the outset. Administrative decision is not infallible (for unanimous confirmation ask any ten faculty members or any one hundred students selected at random) but, within reason, it is usually understood and even forgivable. Completely unforgivable, on the other hand, is the failure or unwillingness of anyone in an administrative position to recognize that he has made an error in judgment and thereby to assume a posture of personal inflexibility. This becomes particularly critical when such inflexibilities affect the total institution; then the result is a moral abdication of the investiture of authority.

Viewed from two different angles, the chief executive officer's line of responsibility focuses at the center of two sorts of decisional differences: those involving questionable judgments made by administrative colleagues and those which he takes upon himself and which turn sour either immediately or some distance down the road. In either case, of course, he cannot escape the final accountability and should not expect to, even when surface evidence seems to indicate otherwise. But pragmatic and unyielding defense, in the absolute, of either the decision or of the person who made it can do irreparable harm to institutional morale and to personal relationships essential to institutional advancement.

The admission of one's own decisional mistake is even more institutionally critical and more personally difficult, especially when one's track record has been pleasantly high for a period of time. One of the risks of the acceptance of an invitation to leadership is that there can be no realistic choice between protection of self and protection of the integrity of school or college.

Decisions aren't forever. Many times, and with understandable tenacity, they are made as if they were to hold a constant validity for the life span of an institution; indeed, for perpetuity, because much of the strength of the implementation of an important decision is its acceptance as one of permanence. For example, a successful change in basic graduation-requirement policy depends upon such change being effected in an atmosphere of confidence and determination. If the horizon of achievement is clouded by a common feeling that the new arrangement is only temporary, then the "bold, new move" can become a timid, feeble exercise of "wait and see."

The same combination of courage, determination for betterment, and hours of planning and decision which initiated the change can again be employed to move forward in another "permanent" direction if conditions so dictate. Decisions aren't forever, because people and programs and problems aren't forever, but plans must be made in recognition of the strength of positive action. They must be carried out within the positive climate of academic adventuring. Although mistakes will be made, people and institutions cannot function in a new program if they are thinking more about the possibility of a mistake than about the opportunities and challenges which the change has presented to them.

Planning for Whom?

As administrators who are now, or who have future aspirations to be, in positions of institutional leadership, let us consider the students once again. They deserve more consideration than we have given them, of late if not historically. It is to our discredit that they have had to shout at us and to enlist the aid of certain elements within the faculty and the citizenry in order that we might, perhaps for the first time in a long time, put them at the center of our planning where they belong.

Regents, trustees, and school boards have been, it seems to me, more aware of this vacuum in planning than have many administrative people. Perhaps this has been because of board members' unique perspective, traditionally once or twice removed from institutional operation. As they become increasingly involved in nonfiscal matters and more actively engaged in policy which *directly* affects students, it is essential that their perspective be retained. A chief executive who does not himself recognize the importance of student-oriented planning can hardly expect to see it in his board. One of the chief administrator's main responsibilities is to ensure planning and decision making of this sort. A good portion of the power which lay boards vest in the president or the principal or the superintendent should be used to double back, to make certain that boards realize the magnitude of the authority they have delegated and that they share a responsibility which is nowhere else duplicated in modern society.

What is best for the instructional process, class by class, department by department, division by division and the cross-referential sums of all these segments, *the total school or college?* The pitfalls of planning are many, some conscious, some semiconscious, and some whose recognizable symptoms are totally submerged until it is too late—too late for the good of the student or teacher or both. Expediency, cowardice, superrationalization, self-interest, building or preserving an empire—all of these are hindrant or destructive to the primary reason for the existence of the institution and to the processes of education. Occasionally, they are to be observed in faculty group behavior or in student government; more often they are daily practices in administration. Reasonable and comprehensive planning cannot tolerate such attitudes or actions. Or, speaking more realistically, the chief executive cannot tolerate such attitudes and actions in himself or in his staff; boards should not tolerate a chief executive who permits them.

The individuals who suffer most in situations where these practices exist are those who are directly engaged in teaching and learning. Put another way, the only true beneficiaries of unselfish, purposeful planning and decision are those for whom our educational institutions exist. Teachers and students—with emphasis on the students—must have an optimum and uncluttered atmosphere for intellectual give-and-take. When administrators plan and when boards participate or ratify, there must be an *agent of focus*. The chief administrator must add or intensify this function to an always expanding bundle of responsibilities.

A favorable institutional reputation is continuously sought, protected, and treasured. It can be a fragile thing, even though reputations, favorable *and* unfavorable, have a way of lingering long after the incident or era which brought fame or dishonor. For example, accrediting agencies periodically and momentarily participate in the life of an institution. They come to know specific strong points and shortcomings in a surprisingly minimal period of time. There is no question but that much of an institution's outside and official reputation is built upon a committee report subsequent to visitation. There is also little doubt that while the committee can determine the present situation and can relate it to conditions during a previous visit, it must take the institution's word on planning for the future. It can do nothing else. Once more, the integrity of such planning and the true test of the implementation of such planning, as important as it is for accreditation and for institutional reputation, is of primary importance to the student and to the teacher. Without constant vigilance, a strong institutional reputation can lose its lustre and an ailing situation can worsen considerably without too much official visibility. The teacher and student first feel the aches and fever because they live and work within the animal itself. Planning and decision cannot be a quick and shallow prelude to visitation. If it is, accreditation may be at stake; the life of the institution is on the line.

Good Plans and Good Timing

Experience and observation would indicate that the best of plans are not always launched in the best of times. When one weighs the factors which can affect a decision to proceed with the most carefully considered of programs, one must put great emphasis on climate and on timing. Near-perfect plans have found their way to oblivion or to the archives (let's hope these final resting places are not completely synonymous within our institutions) because atmospheric conditions and storm warnings were ignored. In order that I may be sure to make the specific point, may I again refer to the decisional function of the chief administrator?

Planning is, or should be, a joint activity, especially that planning which is to affect a complete school or school system, but the final decision to launch or not to launch must be singular. This is true even though consensus or majority or unanimity seems to indicate joint decision. As presidents or principals we might feel more comfortable in company, but the final responsibility cannot be multiple. Decisional responsibility of this sort is not easy to live with and seldom enhances popularity. It can sometimes produce a do-nothing administrator. The mere thought of such burdens can also scare potentially fine decision makers away from top administration. Part of the practicing art of leadership is the ability to recognize and to analyze the signs and times and then to decide upon a move to go, stop, or wait. Fortune can sometimes make a hero but, most often, it depends upon his sense of timing and upon his determination of which way the wind is blowing.

We must, I am sure, realize that *perfect* alignment between the right time and the right plan is as rare as ecliptical frequency. It also follows that with any hesitation, the perfect moment is gone. Therefore, it would seem that to base decisions on timing, at least upon perfect timing, is realistically impractical though theoretically sound. Consider, then, the positive possibility of a "decision zone" which is wide enough to permit flexibility and yet narrow enough to prevent damaging postponement. The halves of such a zone can exist on either side of absolute alignment and thus permit a decisional launch which takes good, if not perfect, advantage of tide and current and which has quite reasonable probabilities for success. There is always an "instant of decision," but that instant can come within a comfortable zone of near-predictable achievement. "He who hesitates" is not "always lost"—only sometimes late, sometimes early, and sometimes wrong; but so is to who does not hesitate. The concept of the decision zone can help the odds in favor of a happy matching of plans and of time.

Decisions and Morale

The permanent institutional effects of a long-term, high policy decision are impossible to determine without the passage of time. The response of constituents and colleagues is usually immediate, together with dire or enthusiastic predictions, but the true picture does not reveal itself until days or weeks or months are behind the decision. Many times a decision which proves to make long-term sense and thus creates long-term positive morale is originally met with short-term resistance or hostility. The risk must be run by the decision maker. As important and as fragile as personal day-to-day morale may be, the strength of year-to-year institutional morale must take precedence. The responsibility for both rests ultimately with the person in authority, even when they seem to be in irreconcilable conflict.

A principal or a president or a chancellor must count heavily upon individual good will in order to reach institutional goals. To lose short-term morale need not always mean the losing of long-term morale but, again, the risk is present. For the person in charge to be aware, to be sensitive, to be as informed as possible—these the sphere surrounding the decision should demand and the individuals within the sphere have every right to expect. But beyond these essentials, the decision maker must watch carefully that he does not put the consideration of possible negative morale before the projected positive effect of the decision upon his school, its basic purpose, and its ongoing life.

Perhaps we ought to look at personal morale from another point of perspective—that of the chief administrator himself. His first major mistake is bound to come and will be followed by an unending series of very visible errors. The sooner the first mistake, the better for him, for his colleagues, and for his career. His inner attitude and its outward manifestations as revealed to others must be strong and positive. His relationship to the job and his ability to maximally perform within that job involves the interpretation of two reflections: his own and that of the general constituency.

The causal anatomy of a decisional mistake is not always easy to trace, but we are more interested here in effect than in cause. If a leader allows the grip of guilt, depression, embarrassment, or self-pity to dominate his consciousness, there can be a geometrically progressive negative effect upon the entire institutional scene. His own doubts concerning his ability to make decisions can soon permeate the collective atmospheres of all segments of the school, college, or university. In reverse manner, a show of strength in the wake of error can confirm the leader in his own eyes, in the eyes of his colleagues, and in his continuing position as the chief executive. Perhaps the greatest show of strength in such a situation is quickly and matter-of-factly to admit to fallibility and to then set about the task of remedy. There is healing in work and there is a singular satisfaction in remedial success. These timeless and limitless truths are no less true in high-level administration in Academia.

An effective top educational administrator is much like a good juggler. This is not only because he comes early to the conclusion that he can never manage always to keep all of the oranges in the air at the same time, but also because he has learned to reach down swiftly and deftly for those occasionally dropped and to work them back into the rhythm and pattern of the operation with a minimum of notice. (I suppose one could use the same juggler analogy when citing good business managers, even though they rarely work with oranges.)

Decisions and Reevaluation

Perhaps the term "reevaluation" is not as appropriate to our total consideration as the term "continuing evaluation." It should be assumed that any educational institution worth its salt is being continually evaluated by responsible members of its staff and that such evaluation is being coordinated by the academic officer in concert with the president or principal. Unfortunately, this assumption is wishful thinking in many of our schools and colleges. It takes a good deal of energy to keep up the head of steam necessary for just the daily routine of carrying on. In spite of this, time spent on continuing evaluation—even stolen lunch hours and midnight oil—can make daily operation proceed more smoothly and more efficiently. That head of steam is not irrevocably tied to a life of huffing and puffing in place; it can be used for advancement or a change of direction.

People in education should be as deeply involved in the process of imaginative reevaluation as they are in energetically following an adopted program. Decisions related to educational reevaluation can be as important as those which launched an original project or which started a school, college, or university in an original direction. Reluctance to tamper with a successful program should not dissuade all concerned from taking a close and continual look at ways to make it better. Our old companions time and circumstance can produce strange arithmetic when periodically adding up the effectiveness of a proven achievement. When two plus two make five or three, then reevaluation can at least indicate the necessity for an in-depth review. Each member of an alert and enthusiastic staff should be mindful of continuing evaluation and should be an active participant. The chief executive's *dual* responsibility is to rely *personally* upon reevaluation and then to insure that his or her total educational unit regularly engages in the process.

Decisions Aren't Forever

Executive decisions are not etched in bronze, hewn in oak, or chiseled in granite, no matter how much we would sometimes like to think that they deserve such immortality. Final emphasis on this point will not, I hope, seem to be redundant. Redundancy, under certain conditions, can be interpreted as appropriate reemphasis. This is particularly true when the point is so obvious as to be overlooked or when the persons or institutions involved are tired of looking.

Executive decisions simply do not forever chart a course, nor do they inalterably bind a school or college to an idea or to a set of ideas. "Undecisions," which may discard, shelve, or reverse the decision of a week ago or of several years ago are an integral part of the life of any institution. Undecisions have the advantage of hindsight; they can reflect the tests of time and of circumstance; they provide an established and understandable place from which to begin again.

The flexibility of decision is a concept which the principal and the president and the superintendent and the board must appreciate, for it is they who most often exercise it. They must use it to advance the reputation of the institution for which they are responsible and to promote the educational process for the full benefit of those students and faculty who are in their ultimate charge. Chief administrators should be able to use with confidence the *flexibility of decision* to their personal satisfaction, knowing that it is one of the most powerful attributes in leadership.

VI. Dusting Off the Old Character

WHAT HAS BECOME OF COURAGE, integrity, statesmanship, trust, strength, and loyalty in the daily and routine affairs of educational administration? By any other names, these character traits are just as important—perhaps more so—as in the day when they were in vogue. Clothed in new terminology, it is possible that they have become less easily recognized or considered not to be as necessary to the administrative process. Strength, for example, has come to be interpreted by some as unilateral power or pragmatism. Statesmanship now has a tarnished echo of compromise. Loyalty is too often a one-way street as viewed from either end. Some sort of semantic sorcery has wrung both meaning and content from the traditional descriptive characteristics by which men and women were once measured.

"A rose is a rose," says the poet; the philosopher must add, "until it loses its *roseness.*" The *nature of courage,* to use another example, should be the same, whether we refer to it as intrepidity, resolution, or fearlessness. But when we call it "guts," there is something lost besides Victorian terminology. A president, a principal, a superintendent, or a board chairman needs to retain the traits of tradition. Retaining or at least remembering the traditional terms by which they are described is, it seems to me, of more importance than would casually occur to most of us.

One of the most sought-after monitor jobs in Mrs. Buchanan's fourth grade class at Lincoln Elementary School was the daily wielding of the feather duster. It allowed the chosen boy (more often, the chosen girl) free movement about the room, a precious commodity which Mrs. Buchanan held in near-total reserve. It permitted a period of prolonged absence from lessons, one being able through vigorous yet silent activity to look a great deal busier than one actually was and to usually string out the dusting until the bell rang at three ten.

Books and bookshelves, picture rails, baseboards, the globe, the alabaster vase which held dried leaves and grasses, and a host of additional useful and useless objects needed daily dusting. Among the more appealing of these was a plaster of paris bust of Plato, to which the feather duster was regularly but gingerly administered. So great was the individual and group interest in this particular and critical point in the duster's daily round that class activity came to a near standstill until the over-tremulant monitor had safely finished dusting off the old character. Some years later, rumor had it that while gesturing toward a particularly poor example of sentence diagraming on the blackboard, Mrs. Buchanan had decapitated poor Plato with a single stroke of her pointer. The rumor was never substantiated. Probably nearer the truth was a later report that it was a combination of old age, seasonal dampness, desiccation, and an allergy to turkey feathers that dusted off the old character for the last time.

If we dust off the old character, what do we find? Perhaps some valuable traits which have all but disappeared through disuse; perhaps a view of the future eyed through the long-empty sockets of a Plato or a Ralph Waldo Emerson. We have lost the old terminology with which to describe the traits we should seek to preserve. It is my hope that in the process of semantic evolution, we have not lost the traits themselves.

What Sort of Person?

We often confuse the question, "What is the president like?" with "What does the president do?" Everyone knows that the presidency requires a set of credentials, a certain platform presence, a facility for articulating the goals and standards of his institution, and an ability to speak Academese like a native. These things can be read in a biographical sketch, heard in an interview, and observed over the first weeks and months of a new administration. But what is the president really like? What sort of person, truly, is the superintendent? It takes more than time to find out: It takes fire and frustration and first-hand dealings with the man or woman in the role of chief executive. Unfortunately, when an institutional leader is hired from outside the family, his performance does not always measure up to the promise of his folder and his interview. Likewise, boards, students, faculty, and staff cannot always expect the same sort of personal reflection from good old Professor X or Dean Y simply because he puts on the mantle and picks up the mace. Incidentally, and still semantically speaking, the new MACE can do a great deal toward reducing any president to a common human denominator, which is probably a good thing because he can always use the sleep and the humility.

We can quickly get to the nature of the person in authority when we observe him in unusual circumstances, circumstances of special stress or of long-term pressure, circumstances of high excitement and of high satisfaction over a job well done. The ways in which he reacts to these situations can best reveal the sort of *person* he is. This is not to be confused with a role he is playing or the operational screen behind which he sometimes hides. How he meets disappointment, tragedy, defeat—how he mirrors personal accomplishment and shares institutional joy—both give simple and accurate testimony to the real person. The person who is, after all, the outward personal reflection of any school or college or university.

Another measure of the manner of man or woman at the helm is what we might call life-attitude. It is more than style, because it is both spontaneous and innate. It can be—let us hope that it is—completely positive. One of the manifestations of a positive life-attitude is a sense of humor. Science might disagree, but it seems to me that a sense of humor can be every bit as traceable to chromosomes and genes as an ability to draw or to sing or to easily throw one's thumbs in and out of joint. Those endowed with the capability to see humor in the midst of crisis are fortunate indeed. Those who serve with a chief executive so endowed may not always agree with him, but they have an important window through which to view him as a person.

If we try to look at ourselves as the sorts of persons who consciously lead and so unconsciously inspire, we should also try to look at those who follow with deepest respect and admiration. In most situations, it is more difficult to follow than to lead, particularly in a profession where intellect and sensitivity are common to all participants. Those who are responsible for moving an institution should place highest personal priority on being worthy of those who follow. And if they can truly follow us as persons rather than the offices which we hold, then advancement has meaning far beyond mere institutional distance traveled; it can mean that people have truly traveled that distance together.

Power and Purpose

In days both misty and musty, chief administrative power was nearly total and usually immediate. Perhaps, in some situations, it still is, though I would hope that history will show us that an evolution away from regentary pragmatism has been a positive evolution. Power is officially vested, but it is more realistically earned, after the fact, through performance. The cold, legal power which the board bestows can fortunately be transmuted to warm, human strength which the entire institution appreciates and respects. Power is granted; strength is proven. If a man's purpose becomes an institution's purpose, he can use strength and power interchangeably and to total positive effect. If his purpose begins or remains as selfish purpose, then he can never differentiate strength from power and can never know the exhilarating feeling which can result from knowing that his purpose is to serve those who must depend upon his wise and cautious use of both.

There has long been talk of the eventual disappearance of the chief educational unit administrator. Principals and presidents, say some, are as archaic as the one-room schoolhouse and the one-furnace college in the one-horse town. Decision and governance by committee; freedom to set one's own schedule and do "one's own thing" regardless of its effects upon others; professional inter-association through the exclusive media of love and good "vibrations"—these activities, at the center of educational process, would allow lofty principles without the need for principals and establish appropriate precedents without the need for presidents. Perhaps. But I doubt if group perspective can be as sharp as singular perspective. And I wonder if committees can ever lead; if ultimate responsibility to a board can ever be shared: if a team made up entirely of quarterbacks can ever handle joint authority and unity of purpose. A school or college made up entirely of students, teachers, and custodians could undoubtedly function. Whether such institutions could move, change direction, or develop necessary auxiliary programs without general administrative support and without chief administrative drive is, in my judgment, seriously doubtful.

A Matter of Stance

The Old Character stood for some things and against others, once in a while inflexibly so, but we cannot blame him. For bending was not a conscious part of his understanding of his charge. In our over-whelming penchant for a working democracy and our all-consuming concern for everyone's happiness in his work, we may have lost or obscured some of the places where it is still necessary to stand. When the chief executive takes a stand, it is interpreted as an institutional stand. And rightfully so. Here is final authority saying it out loud. Not that a stand is universally accepted, or that it is even right. But the chief administrator alone can represent the total internal con-stituency, and he alone can interpret to the public the institutional matters which require standing up and standing for. Hopefully, he recognizes this as an intrinsic professional responsibility rather than some sort of regal right which has descended upon him by divine succession.

The president or the principal, in days present as in days past, must stand *above* some things. For example, he cannot participate in the petty intrigues and the small, personal power struggles so common to the realm of Academia. There is no safe or honorable ground here. An awareness is difficult to escape, even on a large campus, and some knowledge of problem pockets is essential, but direct *participation* by the man or woman in authority can only deepen the intrigue and intensify the struggle. If pettiness begins to blossom into full-scale war or into a situation which can weaken the entire institution, then the chief is automatically and immediately involved. Meanwhile, and

I know we need only to be gently reminded, our tendency to react as humans and to get ourselves into the middle of a small-sized personal scrap should be guarded against. It has happened and will continue to happen to all of us, but perhaps we can learn from The Old Character. He had more important things to do. And so should we.

One foot firmly planted in tradition, the other always probing for a toehold into a new area of experience—this has been the American academic tradition. Change always involves carrying a part of the past into the future. If the best of the past is preserved in the process of change, then it can greatly enhance the chances for the success of an innovative move. I'm not sure that the process of change is always a conscious one; many times educational innovation comes about because of influences completely outside an institution or system. We have probably more often *reacted* to outside influences with so-called innovative programs than we have *acted* in initiating a new program. Whether we are considering review, overhaul, or complete change, motivation should be internal. In this regard, the chief administrator cannot assign or delegate the primary responsibility to see that it is done. The two basic ingredients for educational balance, tradition and innovation, are timeless. The balance is often a fragile and a delicate one. The Old Character knew this and, using his stature and stance, he put all of his energy and imagination to *work* to insure that novelty, fad, superficiality, and caprice were not factors of influence in upsetting educational balance.

Loud and Clear

The "old man's" constituencies knew exactly where they stood with him and he with them. Students, faculty, staff, and those tangential but important individuals and groups outside the operation had no difficulty in receiving the messages or in determining the attitudes of the man who sat behind the big limed-oak desk. His popularity, or lack of it, was not achieved by catering to any or all groups within his sphere of influence. Indeed, popularity was not a consideration any more than it should be in any other time. Respect, yes, and respect was earned.

Courage in leadership does not always rally smiling, enthusiastic followers. If only we could always summon the ability *and* the courage to make ourselves universally heard and unmistakably clear. The problem, it has always seemed to me, is not *how* to be heard or *how* to make oneself clear—rather, it is to cast aside personally the projected uncertainty of the way in which others will react. If the message is one which tells of presidential decision, then it should be stated as simply and as sensibly as possible, with the hope that it will not go unheeded or be misunderstood. If the message is one calling for participation by others, then the projected integrity and strength of the chief executive, together with the clarity of his position, become critical to acceptance and to eventual success. Followers can sense courage; they can also smell fear. The president and the trustees; the principal or superintendent and the school board; and the unique relationships between these individuals and groups need to be viewed from both sides of the table by both "halves" of the whole. An appreciation of the role of each is not always as clear as we might expect or would wish.

It is surprising how relatively little communication takes place between the members of a board and the man or woman whom they have selected to lead the institution and in whom they have placed immeasurable responsibility to carry out daily their legal responsibilities and philosophical purposes. So-called "workshops" for board members; manuals for and memos to trustees; indoctrination sessions for regents—all of these help to create a general but superficial knowledge of what board-executive relationships and joint activities should be. Yet presidents, chancellors, superintendents, principals, and board members cannot come to know each other or to know how they can guide their schools or colleges until they begin to *work* together.

The Old Character and his board knew their relationships to each other. The reading of old board minutes (which becomes more difficult as the reader progresses chronologically from the date of founding) reveals a simple, straightforward working relationship which is to be envied. True, times were more simple and unpretending, but the problems were as monstrous, if not as complex. The president and the board seemed to have had an "attitude-in-common." An attitude which reflected mutual respect and loyalty, dualistic courage and resolution, and a comfortable feeling of trust, which can only come through facing defeat and triumph *together.* We need to use our energies and insights periodically to test whether such a working relationship has fallen into a coma or has died through neglect or unconcern. Just another inescapable responsibility of the chief administrator.

Yesterday, Today, and Tomorrow

Where is The Old Character? Has he grown hollow and brittle and blown away because his time had come or because some of the things he said or did or stood for were no longer "acceptable" in sophisticated academic company? Is he still around, using new names for old problems, or are the problems so different that his kind of courage, integrity, statesmanship, and loyalty can neither confront nor conquer the challenges of the New Academia? Can we still look back to him for reenforcement of ideas, or are the new conditions and the new priorities outside his realm of stance and responsibility? Has change really changed, or was his concept of bold and adventurous innovation so very different from our own?

May I respectfully suggest that, for the most part, we have failed to learn the lessons which The Old Character is still trying to teach us. May I further suggest that he is still around, nearly invisible, perhaps, beneath an avalanche of committees and study groups and workshops and task forces and internships and sensitivity sessions and . . . and . . . and. Quick, somebody, the feather duster!

As we go through change—ever-present, ever-pressing, inevitable change—there are some things which must remain with us in transition, and on the other side: honesty, trust, strength, clarity of purpose. Perhaps you would appreciate knowing that upon Mrs. Buchanan's retirement from the faculty at Lincoln Elementary School, her fourth grade class and the Ways and Means Committee of the P.T.A. presented her with a miniature bronze bust of Aristotle. The change in size, subject, and material really didn't matter. The Old Character smiled and went back to work.

VII. The Teeth of the Gale

ANSWERING TO THE PUBLIC is, finally, up to the school official in authority. Whether the causes for answers are negative or affirmative, it is once again the *personification* of an institution which can be rationally interpretive. The physical college or university or school—bricks, concrete, glass, real estate, ivy, coffee cups, and parking lots—cannot engage in the exchange of ideas. The *real* institution—students, professors, books, thoughts, expressions, curiosities—can speak and can be spoken to. And it matters not if the principal or the president prefers not to be the chief spokesman. He or she is. We are. We must clearly understand this responsibility, accept it, and do everything within our power to deal affirmatively with the external interpretation of the total institution to those persons or groups "out there" who constitute potential threat to or support for our schools and colleges. Hopefully, we will go about it with the firm conviction that the greatest of criticism always contains the greatest of opportunities to turn negative thought or action into attitudes of positive institutional interest and assistance.

Ignoring storm warnings is a dangerous and foolhardy business. Provision for a margin of safety in educational administration is just as important as in sailing or flying or in any activity in which outside influences can weaken or destroy. It does not take an intellectual giant (the term happily excludes most of us) to read weather reports or to sight storm warnings, but it takes a wise and prudent person to react to them appropriately and, in a variety of ways, to make his early peace with the elements. A highly developed "early warning system" can make a significant difference in the degree of executive involvement.

The comparative investment in manpower is interesting to think about. If danger signals are recognized and are heeded in time, the effort to be expended in dealing with an external problem situation can be relatively small. If, however, warnings are inadvertently overlooked, inexpertly misinterpreted, or consciously disregarded, then the fight to bring a runaway problem to solution can require monumental expenditures of human energy and inordinate amounts of time. Though sometimes exaggerated, and most often expressed by chief administrators themselves in a "let's feel sorry for each other because no one else does" sort of in-house, club member expression, there can be no doubt but that time and energy are the most valuable and necessarily rationed resources of presidents, principals, and superintendents. "Sweeping up" was once a literal requirement of authoritative administration. We can now spend our days and use our nervous systems in ways more productive.

Consider, if you will, that the *action* required to deal with threatening outside problems and the *reaction* to those which are already out of hand—indeed, may have reached cyclonic proportion—are both *positive* in nature. That is, they require an affirmative attitude and an affirmative state of mind on the part of the administrator-turned-arbiter. If he or she can affirmatively convince the questioner or the antagonist that the question or criticism was unfounded or, just as importantly, can affirmatively recognize that the critic had sound basis for questioning, then the result cannot help but be positive. All will end well. If this proposition has the echo of Pollyanna's propensity toward the prediction of silver linings, it also has the reflection of a power which a young Galilean carpenter spoke about and which has enjoyed two thousand years of catholic recognition. To stand in the teeth of the gale does not mean that one must always turn the other bicuspid every once in a while, one must bite back—but affirmatively, please.

From Whence Cometh Thy Support?

We casually toss off a term, "the public," as if it were an organized, disciplined, and dedicated entity, recognized by the A.A.U.P., the S.P.C.A., and the Diner's Club and accredited by the Western Personnel Institute and the Northwest Association. Moreover, we consciously or unconsciously assume that the public is hostile—or, at best, suspicious. These feelings are, for the most part, not only unfounded; they are predominantly unfair. If we have lost, or are in danger of losing, a segment of the public, then the fault is more often ours than theirs. There *are* positive answers we should have given to individuals and constituencies within the public. There *are* positive steps we should have taken to bring them inside our institutions or to go out among them. But there is no great Army of The Public facing us menacingly across the Plain of Academia. Individuals, perhaps; small groups, perhaps; national movements, yes. But our strongest position is to deal affirmatively with a public which, individually and collectively, has the potential for positive interest and positive support.

Let us be cautious, however, about underestimating the devastatingly negative forces by which isolated segments of society can bring confusion and crippling upon an institution or upon the reputation of an entire profession. Outside factors, though they be operating under the unfortunate "authenticity" of misinformation or marching beneath the banner of righteous though unfounded wrath, can crush a school or college or can threaten a beautiful internal institutional relationship with widespread destruction or death by implosion.

The strength from within, clearly visible to the outside during the calm before a storm, can do much to give a potential adversary pause to consider. If the storm breaks and the confrontation comes, then inside strength is all the more important. Leadership is *responsible* for institutional stance in threatening times, in battle, and in a peaceful return to a mutual postconfrontation position of understanding. Our people and our institutions cannot always and immediately win the point, even when we successfully resist or resolve the cause of conflict. But institutional strength and resolution, in the positive sense, are characterized in the *person* of leadership. With patience and with continuing personal integrity, we shall yet change some minds and garner some additional lasting friendships. An affirmative attitude is required. It works!

Already alluded to, but perhaps worthy of additional comment, are the phenomena of the visible public and the invisible public. The former we can see, hear, react to, and interact with. Friend or adversary, we know that the visible public is receiving the messages, because it responds. That response is not always to our liking, but it gives us a reading. Consider it, but don't worry about it. Speaking again of energy and of its conservation or waste, the futile and exhausting exercise of energy-spending worry, on an invisible and unresponding constituency should be rejected without reservation. *Development* or *cultivation* of an invisible public is quite another consideration. Save that energy of concern and turn it into an energy of building.

How many representatives of the ghost public can you bring into visibility, and thus into possible support, if you decide to do so? Where are they? They are not unknown, most of them, only invisible. They are townspeople, neighbors, former students, parents, and many more who are close enough to the institution to cast a positive shadow. The adventurous school or college, in reaffirming its purposes or, perhaps, making them externally known for the first time, will bring a reaction from the public. With reaction comes visibility and the opportunity for the sorts of conversations which can be of lasting benefit to the chief administrator and to the institution.

Interpretation Without Misrepresentation

The outside constituencies, if they can be expected to understand and to help, must know more about the institution than its geographical location. They must know, certainly in a general way, what directions the school or college is taking, what ideals and purposes it espouses, what it stands for and, perhaps most important, what it is "up to." Representation to the outside is difficult for those of us in professional Academia. Constantly forming and reforming, academic theories and practices make a concise and consistent institutional reflection all but impossible. Within an atmosphere of increasing demand for "accountability" among voters, legislators, parents, donors, and budget committees in both public and private sectors of education, the task of accurate and positive interpretation becomes more critical to institutional life than ever before.

Any argument over whether these "outsiders" have a *right* to inside knowledge is, begging both your pardon and the question, academic. Perhaps the private school, college, and university have a more defensible position in regard to the prerogative of keeping things in the family, but the net effect of the sustaining or discontinuance of understanding and support is principally the same. What the institution is "up to" is certainly its business, but it is no longer exclusively its own business. The interpretation of that business by its chief administrative officer must not be misrepresented. Faculty, staff, students, even board members, can be forgiven for speaking about school and college without all of the facts and the clarifying background, but the chancellor, the superintendent, the principal, and the president speak *as* the institution.

Accurate representation cannot only be expected; it can and should be demanded. This is not to say that a chief administrator has no choice but to reveal his school or college or university as an open book to each and every constituent, inside or outside, friend or foe, rational or unbalanced (and who can always be sure?). There is a process of selectivity in reports on school activity. Moreover, the concern for "family" and the compassion for individuals within does not always permit wholesale distribution of details without. Perhaps the public deserves to know, but providing general information about institutional direction, financial position, and academic responsibility does not mean that curricular, budgetary, and philosophic details *must* be shared with everyone who asks for them.

No matter which end of a horse the chief administrative officer is presumed by some to be, he still speaks for the institution. And final satisfaction is not realized by those asking the questions until they hear the answers from the horse's mouth, which fact alone should clear up any equine anatomical uncertainty. If this is true inside the institution, it is even more so outside. When he responds, an honest and straightforward presentation can build confidence and support even when the answer he gives is "bad news."

Everybody's Business

Anything that happens within a school or college, or to individuals
or groups connected with it, becomes of greater or lesser interest to
some segment of the public. If it is an achievement of which we are
proud and which we feel should receive publicity and it doesn't, then
we are resentful and accuse the news media of overlooking the positive news and of being interested only in the sensational. If, on the
other hand, a campus incident is negative or threatening, then we
resent its receiving any publicity at all. In the latter instance we call
it "family business" and complain at its becoming public property.
Either way, no exasperated school official has ever had the last word
in what always proves to be useless debate with the news media over
what constitutes news or whether the reader, listener, or viewer has
the right to know.

News is news to a newsman. And yet, with only one or two exceptions, I have always enjoyed a mutually respectful relationship with
the ladies and gentlemen of press, radio, and television. What possible good can come from continual complaining about the inclusion
or exclusion of campus news stories? We purport to know the essentials of our profession; we ought to assume that the newsman knows
his. Our personal and institutional imaginations, energies, and moti-
vations should concentrate upon the creation of *good news* and upon
favorable institutional representation to the public. Whether such
good news is in the form of an interesting or informative announce-
ment originating within the institution, or whether it neutralizes or
counteracts an unfavorable story originating with the news media,
the attitude of the appropriate faculty member or administrator and
of the chief executive must be one of open-mindedness. The final
result is almost certain to be positive, and no hard feelings have pre-
influenced the next encounter. As in football, the best defense is a
good offense. Positive and amiable attitudes can do much to pull some
of the sharpest teeth from the mouth of the strongest gale.

One on One

In meeting criticism from or in projecting positive action to the public, the most effective means, of course, is to use the proven technique of person to person. Isolating a problem, clarifying a question, proposing an explanation, admitting an error: convincing, explaining, defending, arguing, agreeing, reaching mutual understanding. All of these vital exercises in human relations affecting our schools and colleges can never be totally accomplished by "messages" in publications, by holding mass meetings, by arranging appearances before community and civic groups, or by making statements to the media. No great or original revelation this, but it is my observation that most of us, as those who are or would be chief administrators, let too many *one-on-one* opportunities pass us by. We hide behind paper work, committee meetings, and an appointment schedule which prevents us from getting out from behind the desk and *making* one-on-one opportunities.

Declaration of an opinion or loud defense of a personal or an institutional position usually has no real power other than in terms of decibel level or of type size. More than this, we tend to declare and defend in the Academian tongue whenever we have an audience larger than one. Two people in discussion can never have an impersonal experience. Whether or not understanding takes place cannot be assured; it depends upon the people and upon their hoped-for affirmative attitudes.

There is another important reason for using the technique of one-on-one discussion. Something measurable always happens. Perhaps results are not as either party would have wished at the outset; perhaps no real convincing has been accomplished; perhaps only a perpetuation of deadlock has taken place—but all of these are measurable. Upon measurement, positions can then be reevaluated, new channels can be opened, compromises can be considered. This is not possible with a declarative opinion directed to an audience which cannot engage in the give-and-take of personal discussion.

If we look at this *one-on-one* activity from the view of the involvement of personal feelings, we must again arrive at the conclusion that it is worth the effort. With an affirmative attitude on the part of just one of the participants, the experience will bring personal reward. Because win, lose, draw, or "none of the above," two people have engaged in conversation which can eventually strengthen them as persons. To strive for personal growth is always of mark, and to strengthen the person of the chief administrator is to strengthen the institution he has chosen to serve. Thus what would seem to be semi-selfish motivation in the personal development of an individual becomes a critically unselfish by-product which will lend itself to a better school or college. As ordinary mortals, we cannot, and cannot be expected to, always "put the institution first." We can, however, always be sure that we put our personal positive attitudes first and allow the resultant outward appearance to look the public, singular or plural, right in the eye.

Minus-to-Plus

The worst possible situation, personal or institutional, contains plus factors and seeds of promise. I believe it. This is not to realize that wrongs will always be righted, misunderstandings resolved, and mistakes corrected automatically or by the grand wish. It is to realize that the elements of positive promise are indisputably present and that they are wholly subject to the attitudes of the *persons* involved. The public, because of its diverse and multiple nature, cannot act as a person in the beginning stages of the correction of a minus situation nor can the institution. Minus-to-plus begins with person-to-person. The basic requirements for the initiation of the minus-to-plus process is for the leader of the institution to *believe* it can be done, act as if he believes it, and recognize the need for closely charting its progress. And progress it will, for the eventual acceptance of an ever-widening group of people and to the satisfaction of both public and institution.

The gates to many fine private schools and colleges have been permanently closed because of a lack of confidence in their projected future and a lack of belief in their top leadership. Many tax-supported institutions, elementary through university, have suffered similar near-total setbacks, even though increased tax levies and legislative appropriations or burgeoning enrollments have kept most of them open. The plus factors, the seeds of promise, are in the minds and in the physical energies of men and women who search for, find, and *use* the available positive factors in a seeming storm of negativity.

Automobiles are designed to start in "neutral," but in the early days of the horseless carriage, when a person rather than an electrical device was the starter, the neutral gear sometimes slipped and the man at the crank might be threatened with bodily injury as the engine whirled into action and the vehicle charged forward. Or if the reverse gear had been left engaged, a fence, a member of the starter's family, or the house across the street might be endangered.

"Neutral," the desired condition for starting, described a condition that reflected both the comfort and the safety so necessary to the situation. From a position of neutral, a shift to an action gear was necessary for advancement. On many early model autos there was no reverse gear. I have known presidents and principals with no reverse gear. Too bad, because backing up can sometimes be as important as moving forward and can be just as positive.

Where, we should continually ask ourselves, does minus end and plus begin? The mathematician or the philosopher could construct a formula or an equation which might be of some help. But for those of us who were permitted only to see Pythagoras as through a blackboard, darkly, the simple proposition that the *moment of plus position* begins in the mind of him or her who *believes it has come*, will have to do.

Reassurance and Pledge

Any school or college should be a vital, vibrant entity. It lives and it can give life. It has its moments of failure, of frustration, of crisis; but it also enjoys respect, affection, and good will, as do all humans and human institutions. It will always be alternately vulnerable to criticism and deserving of praise. In most instances, it receives exactly what it earns. External exposure is not only necessary, it is essential to the life and to the life processes of the institution.

The chief administrative officer must accept the responsibility to *guarantee* that such external exposure takes place. He must also be ready to accept, with courage or humility, whatever comes. He alone has the authority to voice the justification for the existence and the total purpose of the school or college he serves. He must be a person who can stand strong in the teeth of the gale, believing that his institution is indestructible and that his people are the greatest to be found anywhere. The public wants to hear this more than anything else.

VIII. The Eye of the Hurricane

THE PRINCIPAL'S OR THE PRESIDENT'S OFFICE is "where the buck stops." Perhaps there are active trustees or regents who would take exception to this declaration (after Harry Truman), but in the daily activity of the ordered and organized affairs of men, final decisional responsibility presents itself, in person or in writing, to the chief. One of the best examples of this is to be found within the Kingdom of Academia, where institutional life and life-style might differ from other areas, but where internal anatomy and life processes are substantially the same. In any organization, the chain of command or *the chart* delineates or unmistakably implies administrative responsibility up and down the line. If detailed job descriptions are also a part of the written plan of operation, then decisional limits can be spelled out to correspond to the squares and lines on the chart. Fine. However, in spite of this delegative, logical, scientific symmetry of purpose and poetry of intent, the chart and the description are meaningless beyond a certain point. Regardless of the intelligence, capacity, and dedication of the occupants of the squares on an organizational chart, they *cannot* and *cannot be expected to* take the total responsibility for decisions which involve the complete operation or to respond with authority when the soup reaches a certain thickness or when the wicket gets a little too sticky.

The office of the chief administrator can and should be a place where calm appraisal can help determine a course or precede a decision. Of recent years, technological advances have given us computers, data banks, retrieval systems, management surveys, utilization studies, accountability reports, and a host of nonhumanistic influences which can be both threatening and reassuring. We must always take careful cognizance and make cautious interpretation of what these racks of metal and stacks of paper have to say to us. For many.

73

they seem collectively to offer a sort of electronic enigma which presents itself to ordinary mortals as a coded and therefore unintelligible reel of tape, or a silent row of staring eyes smug with their own secrets, or a pleated paper print-out which joins the road map as being humanly impossible to fold back once unfolded.

These are things which the traditionalist is tempted to flee rather than to befriend. But, even as we contemplate direction in the calm of the center of the storm, they can render mechanical assistance in the final human exercise of decision. If we do not allow ourselves to become intimidated by the sights and sounds of these purveyors of sterile fact, we can be materially assisted by the data which they provide. There should be no philosophical conflict here, only reasoned judgment as to the limitations of solid-state answers which follow philosophical questions in less than one ten-thousandth of a second.

Perhaps time has caught up with the traditional luxury of the lengthy weighing of alternatives and contemplation of a variety of possible results. But the chancellor and the superintendent and all persons in positions requiring ultimate educational decision must preserve an atmosphere of deliberate objectivity in times of crisis, for the long-term preservation of their institutions and for the short-term preservation of themselves. The "eye" of the hurricane which, until recent discovery proved quite the contrary, was historically considered to be the frenzied, turbulent nucleus of storm activity. Investigation showed, as it so often does, that theory was wrong, that the center of the storm was, in reality, an antivortex; a tunnel of calm where observation, consideration, and prediction about the extent, magnitude, and movement of the storm could reasonably and rationally be accomplished.

We have often considered institutional health like an anxious mother. Let us again consider personal health, specifically the mental and physical health of those persons who carry the basic burdens of institutional responsibility. A sick principal means, for example, the distinct probability of an ailing or a "holding" school. Not that trusted lieutenants, close colleagues, and eminently capable associates (our hope would be that all of these descriptions would fit the second-line officers of any school or college) cannot carry on in the absence of an indisposed chief executive. Not that at all. They can, and we are grateful. Rather, let us remember that a principal, superintendent, or president who has the strength and vitality to *lead* is in a position to make effective use of the talents and strengths of his associates, adding them to his own to move the institution.

To *preserve* a climate of calm and to *demand* of time that it grant moments of tranquility is to guarantee that one's head and heart and stomach are always ready for the tumbling turmoil of the hurricane. Like the pilot of the first aircraft which flew into the center of storm activity, quite probably in fear of his life, *you* will have to discover the "eye" for yourself; *you* will have to work and to concentrate to maintain your internal equilibrium; *you* will and can experience the positive, healthful effect for yourself.

Self-scheduled Calm

One must schedule his own calm. In looking at the most ironclad daily appointment schedule, if one is chained to such, there are still small blocks of time available for calm. But this is only looking at the surface of possibilities. On one's way to an appointment, for example, whether it be eighty-seven miles or eighty-seven steps away, there is *time*:

√ Time to worry about what he will say and what you will say.

√ Time to ponder the long-term consequences of an unsuccessful interview.

√ Time to build yourself a hurricane.

√ Or time to schedule yourself a piece of calm.

Granted, it is difficult, but the mental, yes, and the physical, exertion necessary is worth the effort. The result will afford a condition which will produce the required lucidity, creativity, and wisdom when they are called for. Many times the hurricane blows itself out before the moment of crisis we have talked ourselves into is reached. Many times the dreaded or anxious hour upon which we think the whole college or university will falter or fail never arrives, not because we have remained inert but because calm has licked tempest.

Because the eye of the hurricane has revealed itself to be a tunnel of self-renewal and of new confidence.

To fight oneself within the eye and to stay there until patterns emerge, insights are gained, and total calm is restored takes much self-imposition and much balance. At first, it is difficult to keep oneself right side up or even to recognize which is right side and where is up. It is difficult to focus on the inside while a continuously revolving blur is distorting the outside. It is difficult to *concentrate for calm*. We need to remember, however, that both concentration and calm involve power. Power is synthesized in concentration and it is released in calm. The loosing of calm power is one of the most important aspects of healthy, effective leadership.

Where are we when the hurricane eventually spends itself? Though it would often seem that stormy conditions are continuous, we know that in one way or another, singular storms pass. True enough, they perpetually come upon us in an endless succession of waves. The weather segment of the five-thirty news informs us that even though "Alice" is dissipating her force in the Florida Keys, "Betty" is gaining strength and heading for the coast of South Carolina. Where are we between storms or between the peaks of the cycles of storms? Do we stay in the tiger's eye and ride her down or do we sometimes end up as derelict debris, deposited capriciously far from home by an airborne whirlpool? Presence of mind in the midst of a storm or disciplined self-renewal between a never-ending series of storms can be powerful, logical, exemplary sources of strength *if* we put power, logic, and strength into them.

Deadeye and Dame Fortune

More years ago than he now cares to remember, a small boy persuaded his grandfather to take him to a carnival. It was one of those itinerant boy-traps which played in dubious concert with county fairs and agricultural farm-implement displays, and whose dingy banners and sandpaper-tonsilled pitchmen extolled wonder, excitement, and opportunity. The wonder and excitement did not even require advertising; the Ferris wheel and the tumble bug clearly spoke for themselves. The opportunity was to be found in the games of skill or of chance. It was 1933 and in addition to either popcorn or cotton candy, the boy had another choice with his other dime. Three successful shots with a .22 caliber rifle, possible even if the sight was missing and one's trigger finger was slippery with popcorn butter, could win a bag of marbles, a plaster-of-paris statuette of Popeye or Betty Boop, or a genuine alligator-hide wallet. The boy's grandfather gently reminded him that he was a pretty good shot with a .22. On the other hand, if the Wheel of Fortune stopped on exactly the right number, the prize was a real, live puppy. Three chances for a choice of three prizes or one big chance for one big prize. It would be a temptation to relate that long and serious deliberation took place before the boy reached a decision, as had been the case with the popcorn and the cotton candy. No such thing. He unhesitatingly presented his shiny dime to the sweaty man behind the canvas counter and received a limp, damp ticket in return. Number five. The click of the leather strap on the nails, the motion of the turning wheel, the near-vertigo from trying to find number five among the blurring digits until the wheel had slowed, the combined feelings of humiliation and despair when it became obvious that number five would be half a wheel away from a winner—sights and sounds and smells and whirling activity unified to make a sick and heartsick eight-year-old. I wish I could tell you that the boy completely learned his lesson. He is a little wiser now, perhaps, but he is still drawn to the hollow promises of the barker and the come-on man. Perhaps to see if he is still a fair shot with a .22, perhaps to spend twenty-five cents to try to accomplish something that a dime could never do. But more probably to take his gastronomic chances with a couple of totally predictable "sure things." A bag of popcorn *and* a swirl of cotton candy.

Make time. Take time. Take time to be right or wrong or confused. Lady luck plays a great part in our administrative lives, but don't make it difficult for her or put the odds beyond her reach. Influence her; prepare for her moment; don't put all your dimes on number five. If circumstances dictate that you personally shoot from the hip, be ready to accept the consequences personally. History doesn't really care because, one day, even popcorn and cotton candy are gone.

Who Established the Educational Establishment?

Have you ever wondered about the first true administrator? We cannot really count the venerable founder-president-teacher-money-raiser who came by administration unnaturally. Since it is safe to assume that the president had no contract or no "understanding" stating that he was not to stoke the furnaces, he either did it himself or, what proved to be a fatal mistake, he designated someone else to see that it was done and thus created the first administrator. When was the first "administration" formed? I suspect that it was an uneasy alliance between the president and the registrar. Not that they did not do most things separately but that they were forced to do some things together. And that meant, for the first time, that "the administration" made some decisions, established some policy, and the educational establishment was born.

Since that signal day, students and, alas, our colleagues-who-teach, have resignedly looked upon the administration as middle-aged, middle-thinking meddlers without whom the institution could blossom into a bower of intellectual beauty. As most of us have grown older, "the administration" seems to have grown more understanding and more relaxed. Some have explained this as a bridge over the establishment gap. I thing it has more to do with our recognizing that there have always been gaps and that there will always be gaps. We've just stopped fighting it. Hooray for gaps! They remind us that people are different, ages are different, eras are different, but that turmoil, controversy, argument, misunderstanding, and other conditions of hurricane force are timeless, and they are a large part of what keeps an educational institution alive. Once in a while, unfortunately or even tragically, as has been the case since the beginnings of education in America, the cause for the turmoil is louder than the case for the argument—and someone starts throwing rocks. When that happens, our first duty is to the physical safety of our charges. But when we can retain our balance in conflict, the chances for opposing ideas to direct themselves rationally and positively toward review and reform are increased both rapidly and geometrically. If we can, *together,* reach the eye of the hurricane, then the establishment and those who feel disestablished can continue the argument within the protective and supportive cone of reason.

The activists have a point or two, you know. They want things to happen. Just as we who have chosen a career of educational leadership want things to happen. Is it any wonder that campuses are often turbulent, that boiling points on societal, environmental, or moral issues are reached in colleges and universities sooner than anywhere else? Give us the turmoil and the turbulence, even the trouble, but also give us the wisdom to count to ten (maybe, these days, only to five) and the courage to fly into the hurricane and to find the calm that is inherently there, in the center of it all.

A Working Objectivity

It is often difficult to see or to respect the other side of a question or of a controversial issue. Many of us have mourned the decline and near fall of interscholastic and intercollegiate debate because of the things it teaches with subtlety and indirection. One must *work* for objectivity, usually thought of in terms of seeing each side or, perhaps more realistically, admitting that there just might be another side. Leadership, however, demands a third dimension in objectivity. Men and women in authority must see *each* side and must then see *both* sides. This calls for a peculiar sort of vision, not always appreciated or understood by colleagues. By way of illustration, do you remember Aunt Mabel's stereoscope? Holding this collector's item up to our eyes for a breathtaking view of Yosemite Falls or the Great Pyramids of Egypt helped to pass many a rainy afternoon. Looking at the double-image card with one eye and then the other, we saw with each a flat, one-plane image. But opening both eyes at the same time produced the "third dimension" and a totally new effect. It is difficult to see both sides at once as opposed to seeing one side at a time.

Looking once again at the *person* who is chief administrator, the eye of the hurricane can provide more than an objective tunnel of rationality in which decisions can more easily be reached and a means by which the rat race may be momentarily held in suspended animation. Healing takes place from the inside, outward. The healing process must begin *inside* the crisis, *inside* the turmoil, *inside* the trauma, *inside* the wound. The process is, in many cases, a natural one, but time is the most important factor in healing, and time is not always in abundance.

We can help time by pushing ourselves inside the problem, where the healing must begin. We can accelerate both time and the healing process by using our own positive attitudes as personal and institutional examples. Some wounds will never completely heal. We know that. But our personal lives and the lives of our institutions move on, and they move on and over and around and through our problems. Acceptance of this inevitability, striving for three-dimensional objectivity, and belief that leadership carries tremendous potential for healing and advancement make the difference between an exceptional administrator and one whose office door carries the designation that a president or a principal can be found inside.

Creeping Doubts

Everyone who ever took unto himself or herself the responsibilities of authoritative educational office has had moments of serious doubt concerning his or her ability to lead. If such moments stretch into lengthy periods of time which result in personal agony or institutional imbalance, the ultimate answer is difficult but necessary. Get out! But before we give up, let's look at professional doubts, personal and impersonal, selfish and unselfish, within the now familiar and relatively comfortable atmosphere of the hurricane's eye. There, one cannot be afraid of doubt. One understands it and respects it. It is easier to grapple with doubt in a private place. Doubt cannot live with light. Doubt cannot live with calm. Doubt can be an ally; only fear is an enemy. When doubt, uncontrolled and abandoned, turns to fear, then it requires massive amounts of physical and mental energy to bring it back into positive focus.

We have hopefully convinced ourselves that we are practicing artists in educational administration. There have been and will be times when uncertainty, not only about that simple proposition but about the ten thousand details of the practice itself, will assume overpowering proportion. This is not theory. This is why elementary principals become textbook salesmen, secondary principals become insurance and mutual fund representatives, college and university presidents become foundation executives, school district superintendents go back to teaching, and board chairmen sometimes decide to become college or university presidents. Doubt seems to be a good part of such decisions. Oh, yes, and frustration, overwork, unappreciative co-workers, developing ulcers, hostile students, longing for the good old days in administration. Your list would probably be better than mine. I wonder if all erstwhile administrators take these conditions, these doubts, with them when they make a change or leave education. Some have expressed to me that they have. More have said that their decision to leave was too quickly made, and made in the maelstrom of overwhelming personal-institutional turbulence or in the agony of self-doubt. Perhaps if all that physical and mental energy had been spent in reaching the center of the turmoil—the eye of the hurricane—we would not have lost so many good men and women to occupations which will earn them a living but which will never provide the strange and wondrous combination of sacrifices and satisfactions which characterize educational administration.

There are at least two things one can do to a creeping doubt : make a lifelong companion of it or step on it.

Please Pass the Buck

When the buck is passed and comes to uneasy rest in front of the principal or the president, it is interesting to view the situation in terms of both the passer and the passee (recent review of institutional-legal relationships has given us a whole new set of descriptive phrases which we can now adapt to the Academian language to further confuse ourselves and the public). The usual interpretation of buck passing is that he who passeth is grateful for the opportunity and that he who receiveth wishes that he could send it back or at least exchange it for a smaller size. Moreover, it is often assumed that once the buck is passed to the highest operational authority, the one who presented it has no further interest or responsibility, and the one who accepted it, with reluctance or dread, is singularly stuck with finding a solution or explanation. These interpretations are, for the most part, unrealistic and untrue.

A superintendent or chancellor, a principal or president who cannot see that *the buck* brings disguised challenges and opportunities is not that rare. It is too easy for the chief executive to feel that his desk is a dump rather than a laboratory. He will eventually speak for the institution but, in the meantime, he will seek counsel and research the background of the cause of the problem. Where better to first seek out and inquire of that colleague immediately responsible for "the last pass"? From the colleague's viewpoint, he cannot erase a sticky situation from his consciousness by the simple act of writing a memo, sending a folder, or pleading and bleeding on the president's rug. More often than not, his specific interest in details surrounding the buck-passing incident is greater than his chief's. He is bound to follow the subsequent progress and, most likely, will play the most important part in the eventual resolution of the difficulty.

It is essential that we look affirmatively upon those situations which appear to be totally negative. Of course they are bothersome, time-consuming, and costly expenders of energy, but we should welcome the opportunity to try to resolve problems, to right wrongs, to heal wounds, and to correct misunderstandings—to practice our chosen art. On the other hand, most boards and students and faculty will make allowances for inaction, tolerate negativism, make exceptions for languishing leadership, understand the administrative maxim that tomorrow will take care of itself for about as long as it takes to get to tomorrow. Why not trade a tomorrow's worth of anguish for five minutes in the eye of the hurricane?

IX. Wisps of Smoke

As IS THE CASE WITH MANY FAMILIES, the chief administrator is most often the last to know about those shadowy goings-on which are a part of the character of every school or campus community and, indeed, of every human institution. There is little he can do about it, for such is the nature of things. When the shadows begin to take on recognizable shapes, however, and when those shapes loom as potential threats to persons or to programs or to purposes in which all have an institutional stake, the president or principal must quickly shift from smoke watcher to fire fighter. The manner in which the chief (in this case, the fire chief if I may be forgiven) conducts himself when eventually confronted with internal unpleasantry and ugliness can affect his personal relationships with those both directly and tangentially involved. Unfortunately, it can also influence internal and external support.

When the chief concludes what action, if any, should be taken, all segments of the institution are subject to an involvement and to a personal position which can create either positive or negative pressure. Those sitting as spectators usually have an opinion edge on the chief executive, because they have been in possession of some sort of knowledge of the situation for some period of time and have, therefore, already made judgments of their own. Whether or not fact or background entered into these judgments makes little or no difference; those making them are always ready to match the action of the person in final authority against their own. Some quickly voice any disagreement, not, alas, with voices which can be heard and answered, but with wispy, smoky voices which, of course, start the entire process over again.

The responsibility of the president or principal is not made of mist or of cobweb; it is as real and as visible as a block of granite. He or she cannot hide or conveniently melt into the crowd when smoke becomes flame. "What is the president going to do?" is the first question and is thought or expressed alike by the puzzled, the outraged, and the condoning. "What action will the principal take?" is the beginning of a questioning and guessing sequence which can turn an entire school or school district from a wisp of smoke into an inferno. Many times, of course, the smoke watcher is able to locate and eliminate the source of unpleasantness without a widening circle of onlookers. But shadow is shadow and smoke is smoke; both attract the immediate attention of human beings and neither is easy to grasp or to hold. Chief administrative participation in such difficult exercises most often reaches a climactic moment in full view of a well-watching if not entirely well-wishing audience. So be it. And so beware.

Very much like his counterpart at Engine Company Number One, the chief cannot spend his entire watch preoccupied with squinting or sniffing after smoke. Moreover, the quick conclusion that all smoke is the indicator or the manifestation of fire can be reasonably questioned. Just as interesting is the posing of the query as to whether smoke or fire or both are always to be suspect, feared, or frowned upon. Educationally or administratively, wisps of smoke can point to situations where flame should not only be allowed to burn freely, but should actually be encouraged. Positive or negative smoke? Constructive or destructive fire? The identification and determination of these alternatives fall within the responsibility sphere of the institutional leader, and they have much to do with the successful practice of his art.

Managerial Myopia

Myopia is clinically defined as nearsightedness, but its treatment by both Mr. Webster and Dr. Roget includes the definition *short*-sightedness. The semantic and philosophical implications are most interesting in terms of our current consideration. The intriguing idea that to be nearsighted can cause one to become shortsighted or that the two terms are considered synonymous is one that invites some exploration. Take the average capable, dedicated, efficient, harrassed, and confused educational administrator as he faces the daily merry-go-round of his responsibilities. Take, specifically, the chief administrator who must delegate a varying amount of detail of his responsibility to members of his staff.

In addition to their roles as independent agents of the institution in regard to certain operational segments thereof, administrative staff members become extensions of the seeing, hearing, and other sensors of the chief. This does not mean, however, that the president or principal should delegate away his eyes and ears and other perceptors "in order to concentrate on the big picture." His nearsightedness is most important in many instances, and when his eyes get tired from alternating rapidly from near to far, he has the comfort of settling into a bifocaled world. Nearsighted and shortsighted are not absolute or interchangeable synonyms. Not at all. They have one indisputable characteristic in common. They can give one an uncommon headache. It is worthy of note, by the way, that both close colleagues and administrative officers of the line completely understand that they are extensions of and not replacements for presidential or principalian antennae.

What if we were to suppose that the concept of eyesight, as philosophically considered here, could be replaced by "mindsight"? This is really what we are talking about within the context of the entire process of perception-judgment-action. Mindsight then goes beyond discovery or revelation; mindsight includes investigation, weighing of fact against fancy, and the finality of either actively or passively dealing with the current status of the wisp of smoke in question. Only incidentally does it happen that mindsight rhymes with hindsight. Fortunately for us, our eyes are located where they are, else we could not see sitting down. That sort of sight is out. Let us put sight in front of us, where it belongs.

Neither can mindsight include true foresight, though the circumstances of fortune sometimes make it appear that we are so equipped. Mindsight begins from a zero position: no predictions, no afterthoughts, no warnings, no close-up or far-away visionary advantages.

It is a *process* rather than a string of reactions and actions. The segments of mindsight are wired in neither series nor parallel circuitry; there is only one segment and it is its own power source and energy cell. It is complete, packaged, and in perpetual use or reserve. It sees, sorts, assembles, and acts. Mindsight is a continuum of influence which only the practicing artist can appreciate.

Janus Is Not Smiling

Janus, that curious, double-countenanced fellow out of Roman mythology, seems to have had no reason to smile as he reportedly looked in two directions at the same time. Whether he was searching for wisps of smoke or glimpses of Venus at the pool, there is no pictured or written indication that he liked what he saw. Janus is not exactly atypical; many times we are not overjoyed when we look around us. Or, we are not too pleased with what we hear when visited by the one-man, self-appointed Grievance Committee and Information Center. Well intentioned or not, the tattletale implications of the "after-five" visitor make many a chief executive uneasy, perhaps reminding him of another day and another situation. Putting aside the immediate disquieting effect and the resultant tendency to build walls, let us hope that we can always see positive possibilities within the framework of, "I thought you ought to know that . . ." People with problems or with potential problems should be protected in many instances, helped in most others. To save a faculty or staff member who has erred but has also shown promise or to save a student who deserves a chance to prove he can overcome his difficulty, these are nearly always preferable to a net loss. Just where the line is drawn or whether saving a person will endanger the good name of the institution is never predictable. And, quite often, the judgment of the person drawing the line proves to be faulty. In the main, however, there are more positive elements in salvation than in damnation, regardless of how the president or principal is made aware of a potential pocket of difficulty.

Why isn't Janus smiling? Artists have traditionally depicted our four-eyed friend as dour in expression. Perhaps he is smiling under his beard. Also, just possibly, it is our fault that he is not the picture of joviality; we haven't given him much to smile about, either coming or going. Perhaps we can do something about it. It would mean that we must give him favorable and positive vistas in at least two directions and also endow him with the peripheral vision necessary to compensate for being able to look forward and backward but not from side to side. Suppose we could summon the temerity to tamper with the symbolism of ancient Rome and give Janus two additional faces. This would not only afford him 360-degree vision; it would mean that he would be permanently eliminated from categorization as one of the two-faced so-and-so's of history.

Would we really gain that much extra vision, or would we simply be making myopia that much easier? We really should be trying to see over the hill in one direction rather than over the edges of our spectacles in four, you know. One consideration is that our newly constructed Janus-of-four-faces would now require a specially built set of "octacles" which, though they might enable him to see in all directions, could not guarantee that he would see with any more feeling, intelligence, or total concern than before. In reality, we might be doing Janus a disservice in the long run, because even though he could read three newspapers and a collection of essays at the same time, he might not find anything that would make him smile. I think it is really a waste of time; perhaps what he really needs is a bottle of aspirin for the headache which he has obviously contracted from looking too hard in only two directions.

Rumor and Reality

Often the smoke gets so thick that it conceals the fragile differences between rumor and reality. Mere suspicions can be ignored while a real personal problem situation begins to outgrow its basis-in-rumor. When a thread of truth is evidenced, then the task of the chief executive becomes active in another sense; he has moved along the continuum of mindsight. Rumor first means that someone said something to someone else about something, at this point a wisp of smoke. Beyond this simple beginning, the complex structures for the telling of stories can take a thousand forms. With each, the influence widens, the plot thickens, and the amount of smoke can reach major proportions. It has always seemed to me that the chief executive has a singularly significant role as he becomes aware of and, of necessity, involved in the checking out and subsequent disposition of particularly smoky rumors. His outward *reaction* can do much to squelch a rumor or to put out a fire. Does he react quietly or with great noise? I can think of instances in which either might be helpful or harmful. Does he react quickly or does he take his time? Either can be effective if he has the choice, and he may be right at least half the time. Can past experience help him as he considers a later, similar situation? Probably not often enough for him to be completely confident. He can, however, react with calm, with a clear attitude of fairness, and with a degree of consistency which is apparent to all. He can be sure of only one thing: His reaction and his action will never completely please those directly involved or those watching. But he must react *his* way. A plateau of respect is immeasurably more important to a chief executive than numerous peaks and valleys of popularity.

The appearance of smoke does not always mean that there is fire in the immediate vicinity. Smoke can drift if the air is set in motion by pressure or temperature. Smoke can remain, suspended, at the site of a fire which has been extinguished or has burned itself out. This unpredictable behavior of smoke depends upon conditions *outside itself* and is both philosophically and realistically apropos to our discussion of school, college, or university internal unpleasantness, rumored or with verification. "Where there is smoke, there is fire" is not at all true in many cases. This should speak directly to the point of suggesting that to look in ever-widening circles for cause is more likely to produce results. When a presidential smoke-following expedition reaches something that is indisputably defined as fire and is defined as the *same* fire from whence came the subject smoke then, and only then, is the searcher and discoverer in a defensible position to verify the smoke peddler's allegation. He or she has found *the* fire. Good luck.

Compassion or Cowardice?

Given : a situation which puts a colleague, a student, or an institution in a potentially unsavory position with both inside and outside constituencies. Where does the chief administrator look for justification for his action as he becomes actively involved in such a situation? One place he must always look is toward his own conscience as he tries to sort out his own feelings, then to define the institutional reflection of them. Some of us use the defensive tactic to the extent that we virtually eliminate all others.

Defending and protecting can be a warm and compassionate human act ; it can also be an unconscious act of cowardice—a selfish method by which we quickly attempt to clean up the atmosphere and, at the same time, remove *ourselves* from the unpleasantness. The latter can easily happen when a president or principal identifies too closely with people that he has begun to think belong to him and who comes to think of the institution as specifically *his*. In an earlier essay, we made the point that a special and unique bond develops between a chief executive and both the people and the institution he serves. One of the dangers of such a bond is that overprotectiveness and over-defensiveness can result. The chief executive goes temporarily blind. And blindness can come from either too much stardust or too much smoke in his or her eyes. Censure or silence? Retention or dismissal? Compassion or cowardice?

The final hard choice between two options must be made for the good of the total institution, and that choice must be made by only one individual. If that choice also protects an individual or a group of individuals so that they may have a second chance ; if that second chance produces a favorable result ; and if, in the process, the chief executive's conscience, self-respect, and institutional respect remain intact, then everybody wins. Highly unlikely, but pleasant to contemplate. Again, we see the absolute necessity for flexibility, control, objectivity, and courage—all in addition to compassion. A tall order for an ordinary mortal. A career full of difficult decisions for mere men and women to make, but no one is going to make them for us.

Sometimes, for a fleeting moment or two, we find ourselves wishing and almost believing that the choice can be put off until tomorrow and tomorrow and tomorrow and that, suddenly, we will be magically free of responsibility to make it. It does not take even one tomorrow to remind us that escape is not one of the options. When a problem "goes away," we can be sure that these rare exceptions simply prove the rule that says people solve problems, that problems do not solve themselves. When we must make a difficult choice which goes against a colleague or a friend, it can help to remember that the institution, which must be considered above all else, is also a living, breathing being in a very real sense and that its active life and its integrity must also be preserved.

Farewell

When rumors prove true, when wisps of smoke reveal the actuality of fire, when the difficult decision for separation has been made and made known to the individual involved, then it is only necessary to bid him farewell; to express gratitude for that positive part of his life which was shared with students, colleagues, and the institution. No evidences of malice, no grudges held or sermons delivered, no fatherly advice, no mirror of resentment, no indication of clinging unworthiness—just farewell. No lengthy justification or detailed rationalization on behalf of the general constituency, no recognition of any internal struggle or taking of sides are necessary or desirable. No acceptance of a petition to reconsider—just farewell. For the chief administrator who must make the choice, and for the student or the staff or faculty member whose life stands to be affected by it, the final, very personal act of separation should be "fare well." We can only hope that what was painfully endured as coals of fire, time will allow to be mercifully remembered as wisps of smoke.

X. A Game Without Rules

A SEVERE TEST OF ADMINISTRATIVE SKILL is that of responsible officiating in an arena where one can seldom pull out the rule book for support. Any administrator in authority who attempts to codify every movement of his people and his institution is ignoring, it seems to me, the innate flexibility of education and of his position.

Inflexibility in operation, characterized in part by a series of regulations, discourages creativity, limits growth, and eliminates the opportunity and incentive for new ideas and new ways of doing old things. Inflexibility in a principal or a president or a superintendent is a silent but effective indication to those who serve with him that he is the living personification of a rule book and that he *rules by rules*. Governance by regulations can be a deceptive device which, in theory, can appear neat and tidy but in reality affords no room to grow and no place to go. The very codification which is designed to free entire segments of a school or college from worry or controversy or preoccupation can become an endless coil or rope which shackles, chafes, and restricts a good portion of inner institutional life and intellectual outreach. What is thought to be a sharp definition of an accepted plan or purpose becomes, instead, a blunted instrument which bludgeons rather than delineates, an instrument that pounds rather than points.

There must always exist, I suppose, the traditional manuals, handbooks, by-laws, articles, and other generationally inherited and historically proven collections of do's and don't's and guarantees. Every chief administrator who has served for more than a month finds himself, on occasion, wishing for a historic reference or a printed precedent. This, again, is the tidy way out. Never mind the reason or the integrity or the time sphere of the regulation; never mind the conditions which existed at the setting of the precedent. There it is,

91

in black and white, for anyone to see. So use it. Or let it be used against you.

The reverse thrust of what was thought to be a forward-looking dictum can be deadly. Written in indelible ink and sealed in laminated plastic, codification has acquired a permanence which its authors or legislators quite probably did not mean it to have. What do we do with a gigantic, out-dated set of regulations? We add to it and make it even tighter. The simplicity, clarity, and, above all, the flexibility that should govern our personal and institutional lives has slowly and disappointingly given way to a Rule Book. The farther we slip from simplicity, clarity, and flexibility, the thicker the Rule Book becomes; the more we govern or are governed by frozen strings of words, the more we give up of what we believe to be the essence of our profession and of our calling: freedom to teach and to learn and to arbitrate the problems associated therewith.

The most successful and most realistic, albeit the most frustrating and exhausting, administration of a school or college, it seems to me, approaches the idea of playing a game without rules. Or, if you prefer, a game with only the most easily interpreted of institutional covenants: security and freedom. Both, under most circumstances, should be guaranteed; both carry tremendous burdens of responsibility. Of course, some of us must live with those ever-essential regulatory admonishments such as *Don't Run in the Halls* or *Shirts and Shoes Must be Worn in the Dining Area*. The remainder of the game, the remaining rules under which it is played are, I think, better left to the personal integrity and the personal capacities for understanding, patience, trust, and flexibility of those playing.

The Object of the Game

It sometimes appears that those who write rules and those who interpret rules are most interested in seeing that the basic object of the game should *not* be carried out. In most books of rules, the object of the game is simply and straightforwardly stated, only to be followed by page after page of what the players must do or must not do in order to carry out the object and, moreover, what they must do or must not do to stay in the game. For example, the object of the game of basketball should be fairly obvious, even to teen-age girls and to those visitors from parts of the world where it is not played: put the ball in the basket! If team A accomplishes this in a manner which earns more points than team B, its opponent, then team A wins the game. Dr. Naismith, who "invented" the game of basketball and who devised the first set of "rules," would probably not recognize most aspects of the game today, but his game objective is still the same and is still *the most important consideration* of those playing it. Put the ball in the basket!

Not wishing to engage in debate on whether evolutionary rule changes in basketball have made it more exciting to play or more interesting to watch, I retreat into the protected and more comfortably abstract confines of the realm of Academia. Our institutions must continuously play by new rules or within new frameworks, principally because of the *nature* of education rather than because of its *design*. The object of the game must come before the formulation of its guidelines and their interpretation. We must not be locked in by ancient rules when change demands to be made. We should not be locked in by rules at all. Institutions must decide their goals and purposes, but these objectives are really ways and means of effectively carrying out the object of the game. If we forget about the how and why of teaching and learning and instead concentrate upon the codification of *rules* for accomplishment; if we spend all of our time on the "whereases" and never get to the "nowtherefores," we are not worthy of our cause and of our charge.

Chief, even sacred, among obligations of presidents, principals, superintendents, chancellors, and board chairmen is that of protecting their institutions against the obscuring screen of regulatory preoccupation. The object of the game is teaching and learning and is not the codification of personal rights, personal guarantees, and personal behavior.

Pronouncement and Performance

Throughout written history we have evidences of pronouncement, prediction, and promise, together with the happy or unhappy resultant performance. George Herman Ruth, as every schoolchild who ever collected bubble gum cards is well aware, exemplified the successful completion of *le grand geste* by belting a self-predicted home run into the center field upper deck at Yankee Stadium. The evidence on how many times The Babe similarly indicated his intention and then humiliatingly struck out is not available to us. But we know that pronouncement is not always followed by related performance. Elephants cannot always cross the Alps, even if the man who orders them to do so thinks they can. The chief educational executive who publicly pronounces that he or she will do this or that in a given situation is on potentially dangerous ground. Such pronouncements can, and probably should, be interpreted as political rather than statesmanlike. "I will not permit" and "We shall never allow" are paint-in-the-corner sort of statements which can cause devastating fragmentation when eventually put to the test. Such statements rule out any possibility of discussion, any possibility of overcoming differences or misunderstandings, any possibility of shading between absolutes, any possibility of taking changes in time and temperature into account.

To tie together and hold together the multifaceted and everchanging climates within which educational evolution or revolution is continuously taking place; to keep personal and institutional attention focused upon the basic purposes for which formal education exists; to ensure that excitement and motivation and combined energies of schools and school systems are centered upon creativity and good sense—the execution of these responsibilities is critical to the health of our institutions and to the life of our chief administrators. They are the sorts of positive and affirmative pronouncements which will enlist the aid of others and which will thus help make predictions come true. "You can't" or "I can't" becomes "We can't." But we *can,* you know. And a pronouncement of "We can," though some might be sensitive to the Ruthian element of boastfulness, has immeasurable potential for successful performance. Who must say "We can" in the only voice which speaks plurally on the campus? The administrator in final authority.

Kill the Umpire!

In those inescapable instances when the principal or the president must assume the role of moderator, he might well consider his opportunity potential as well as his bounden duty. Or, when he must become the interpreter of the written word, he can enjoy rather than despise it. In either case, of course, he is as vulnerable to criticism as any official who ever donned face mask or striped shirt. But just before he is expected to assume his position behind the plate and to signal the start of the World Series is no time for an umpire to question himself on whether he really wanted to be an umpire, after all.

Here, with whistle in cheek, are some helpful hints for referees and umpires who find themselves in the wrong profession. They are more truly exercises in preservational attitude than in adjudicational ability:

√ Be consistent, whether your consistency is good, average, or poor, or if you can't even be consistently poor, don't show up.

√ Don't wait too long to blow the whistle, or if you do, pretend that you had difficulty getting it into your mouth and shout a lot.

√ Develop a sixth sense which will allow you to stay right on top of the play, or if you can't do that, fall down.

√ Don't listen to a fan who expresses a personal dislike for you and for your alleged lack of arbitrational expertise, or if you do, be sure to follow him out to the parking lot and get his license number.

√ Don't get into arguments on rule interpretations with fellow officials, or if you do and are losing, drop down on all fours and look for old contact lenses.

Whether expressed in sense or nonsense, the amount of time and importance given to mediating differences and rendering decisions on rules and regulations can consume virtually the total time of the chief executive if he allows it. Sad to say, some school boards and boards of trustees or regents think they want their top administrator to spend his time in this way. And he does. Pity. It indicates that neither party to this sort of contract fully understands the game plan and, even more disappointingly, the object of the game. No one ever kills the umpire. No one ever kills the chief administrator of an educational enterprise, preschool or postgraduate. He may do away with himself—literally or figuratively—and he may have help doing it. But the frustrations of being in the middle are not cause for suicide.

Being in the middle can allow one to play the enjoyable role of bringing people together or bringing about resolutions of "hopeless" problems. What opportunities this being in the middle can afford us! If we can put out of our minds that we run the risk of an occasional flying pop bottle or seat cushion, then, in the middle, we are free to act as the agent through which agreement and advancement can be achieved. Or equally important, we are free to make the final principalian or presidential *decision* which is many times necessary when irreconcilable debate sets up a wall of permanent opposition or leaves a residual vacuum of misunderstanding which must be filled. Unfortunately, it is not the frustration of being in the middle which most often causes executive abdication; it is the inability to accept occasional failure or permanent responsibility.

Operational Momentum

The same surge of force which creates and initiates an educational adventure can give it continuing momentum. The routine operation which must always follow adventuring can never be quite as exciting but is nonetheless of critical importance. The drive which began the adventure and which made the discovery and which launched the proposal must also sustain the working project. An idea is perhaps a rule within itself; it does not need a manual or a set of guidelines. It carries the strength and advantages with which it was born, and it has the life process to precipitate and to void weaknesses. It can add new dimensions to itself, and it can change direction and purpose. Being the mental offspring of humans gives it a vital quality which, among other things, abhors codification and confinement. It is predictably unpredictable; it requires nourishment to stay alive. It also requires operational momentum. In this latter respect it is especially kin to any chief executive. To *live* an idea and to *live* a continuing responsibility for forward motion require staying power as well as imagination. No one writes the rules or the outlines for this sort of life exercise. They must be inherent within the idea and within the leader. They must be redefined at each moment of their continuing existence. The momentum is of the same stuff as the entity, and to agree with one is to pledge to sustain the other.

Returning to our interest in games and rules, let us consider the positive aspects of the contest. For example, the options open in many given sets of circumstances, the possibility of turning a broken play or a miscue into an exciting and unforeseen finish, or the accidental but happy discovery that a slight adjustment in style or execution can have a lasting and affirmative effect. All of these possibilities are outside the realm of rules; they are dependent upon intelligence, courage, imagination, quick recovery, and an ability to adapt to change in an immediate matrix. They also depend upon confidence and flexibility and unshakable belief that *it can be done*. No one writes rules governing these sorts of possibilities. There can be no regulation number three which proclaims, "You will be confident," any more than there can be a rule number five which states, "You will be imaginative." Positive operational momentum *assumes* a reservoir of inborn or developed characteristics and a worthwhile vehicle. Men and ideas are not easily separated, perhaps because their ancestry is uncommonly common.

When in Doubt, Go for It

Some of us behave as if we are playing in a game in which we are always behind. We act as if we started behind and there is no chance to win in the final moments because the game will never be over. We therefore lose the incentive, the strength, the imagination, and the momentum of what must surely be the most exciting career under the sun. We sometimes set aside or dismiss the plus factors which are present in every life situation and decide that we would rather forfeit than fight. We hide behind the uninvestigated assumption that any possibility of positive action is untested, unconventional, or un-constitutional. The search for positive action is not subject to laws or judgments or verdicts or prosecutions or imprisonments. Where does it say, "Thou shalt not try?"

Adventuring in education often makes its own rules. It is not for faint hearts and predictable punters. Early or late in the game—go for it. First and twenty-five or fourth and ten—go for it. Today's heroics call for versatility, surprise, determination, and luck—go for it. Monday morning will bring its critics if, at times, we fail, but no one can level the only unanswerable question, "Why didn't he go for it?" Some of us spend our entire careers waiting for that one bold moment, not realizing that every moment is only momentary when one is mentally and emotionally ready for the challenge which cannot wait. Continuous preparation goes out to meet the challenge; passive existence waits for it. It is *always* a time for boldness, whether we have days or seconds to initiate a positive action. Go for it!

Both the frustrations and advantages of playing, officiating, or watching our "game without rules" are yet another indication that Academia is not so far removed from the way of life in other sorts of human institutions and enterprises. Interpretation of the game can become more difficult in direct proportion to the number of rules devised or added. If the basic concept and the purpose of the game are acceptable to those involved, then the strength and momentum and flow of ideas should be allowed to carry the institution. If the plans, programs, and purposes are in relative alignment and if the people responsible trust each other, then there can be little doubt that combined imaginations and energies will have little need for little rules.

XI. The Myth of Moving On

THE RATE at which the top man moves from institution to institution—indeed, out of education altogether—is on the increase. Even though finances, local problems, and "advancement" are often given as reasons for leaving, we seldom know the true cause or causes. The call of dollars somehow never lives up to its subtle promises. Problems and pressure are only thought to be left behind. Starting with a clean slate (to employ an indigenous metaphor) often means a backward reflection and a realization of the sameness of the color of the grass. A resourceful leader does not need to move in order to grow; he can grow with a growing situation in which he is a daily participant and, hopefully, in which he is the prime mover. His contributions to a particular institution or system need have no predictable terminal point.

Any given situation can be improved. There is never a point when teachers and/or administrators can sit down and rest or when they must throw up their hands and walk out. I have known principals and superintendents and presidents who set five- or ten-year plans for themselves as they accept the chief administrative position as if to say, "I'll sample the situation and, if I like it, I'll try a little more." This is not only grossly unfair to the school or college and its people; it creates a box in which the chief must tentatively live and from which he expects to emerge periodically and test the weather, leave, or be coaxed back for another term. Family plans and considerations are of great importance in the decision to move or to stay, but so are institutional considerations. To make a date for review or termination as a part of the undertaking of a new position, even though it be subconscious or semiconscious, is to add a negative cloud to the positive horizon of acceptance.

To jump from school to school in search of an Academian Utopia is a contradiction of the very essence of what we know education to be: imperfect. If one has a burning desire to strive for perfection, why not use his or her energy to improve the situation which exists in the place which might need it more than the school or college down the road? A lifelong hunt for a perfect spot will result in lifelong frustration. The irony of running away from the *known possible* and running after the *unknown impossible* has always struck me as a monumental cerebral short circuit.

There is, of course, a time to move on. For most, it is called retirement. For others, it is known as mismatch, shouldn't be, or never was. Otherwise smart men and women have shown a remarkable lack of intelligence and insight in such circumstances. If their colleagues are too timid, their board members are too polite, and their wives do not love them enough (more apropos than *too much* in this case) the time to move on is postponed beyond the reasonable and necessary. Both the individual and the institution are likely to be set back with much suffering and sadness. But rationalization and self-convincing arguments to move when such a move is unnecessary and unwarranted turns logic into cowardice or self-advancement. Dedication to oneself can hardly be compared with dedication to one's personal calling and chosen locus of station.

Leaving Problems Behind

An opportunity causes the telephone to ring or is signaled by the arrival of a letter with no return address marked personal and confidential. We puff up and tell ourselves and others around us that if we make the decision to go it is because of the chance to do a bigger job. How impressed with our own importance we become! Seriously consider the big jobs in education. They are to be found in the classrooms of grades one through five in the elementary schools of the nation. One who considers moving to a bigger or more prestigious position, in higher education, for example, is moving in the wrong direction, I should think. But seldom do we move in the other direction, partly because we would not be happy doing anything else, and partly because no group of bright eight-year-olds would have us.

Only the names and the faces change. The problems are tied to the profession and are eternal. Some of the names and faces must prove to be indescribable blurs to the quickly rising and often mobile young chief administrator. But the problems, ah, they are as clear as ever as time passes. They are probably more clear with each year for they are more sharply reflected in the mirror of yesterday's experience. I have often wondered if that mirror always reflects *people* from yesterday and from yesterday's challenge, people who had a great deal to do with the "promotion" and with the reason that the chief moved "up." I hope that it does, for it would do much to make those who move more comfortable and those who stay more appreciative. Two of the nutrients most needed by principals and presidents are comfort and appreciation. It is a pity that we sometimes bite the hands that feed us.

Familiar names and faces are comfortable, too. They can contain the basic element necessary for the first step in an understanding which must precede all discussion, all decision, all operation: *friend*. Friends can argue, disagree, even oppose one another in public debate, but finally, they are still friends. New friends are also important. New friends are always waiting at a new institution. But one can remain in a single school or college or university for an entire career and make almost as many new friends as if he moves a half dozen times into totally new situations.

The budget, the surplus or deficit, the concerns of students and teachers, the questions from the community, the broken steam lines and faulty air conditioning are all institutionally interchangeable. They have little to do with peregrinational discussion or decision. On the other hand, the *character* of an institution, the *feeling* of a district or system, and the *viscera* of a school or college are the things that should influence men and women to stay or to ponder before moving. They are distinct and separate and important and worth the working life and lives of those who are tied to them. Once again, we must consider people. People who need a principal or president or superintendent who *cares* about them and who *believes* in them. People who care about and believe in *him*.

The myth of moving on has as much or more to do with people left behind as with people waiting at the next stop; it has as much to do with the new opportunities in the old situation as with new opportunities in another place with an unknown institutional character. Contradiction of the positive process of adventuring? Only if one is too tired or too nearsighted to recognize that the highest sort of adventuring can be found at home.

I'll Give It Five Good Years

Predicting the segmentation of a lifetime responsibility implies trying instead of doing. It hangs heavy with the suggestion that one is hedging against like or dislike; against acceptance or rejection; against success or failure. It seems to build a way to escape before the necessity for or the advisability of escape is established. "Every principal or president or superintendent should have a back door to his office" is an oft-quoted phrase (most oft-quoted by those who do not have one) which has been taken by some beyond its singular practicality. Too many have widened the interpretation to mean that we need a back door to our careers, or at least to the institution we have morally, philosophically, and, in some cases, legally agreed to serve. I am against back doors; rather than providing convenient openings for escape, they more often build walls and board up the front door.

A chief executive cannot really achieve or lead in an optimum capacity against a background of predecision or escape. If the written, implied, or unconscious terms of professional administrative employment carry a termination or reconsideration date, the period between acceptance of the position and such termination or reconsideration is nearly always shadowed by the measurement of time. We should be occupied with the measurement of other things. The decision to accept an offer to lead a school or college should not have anything to do with time; it should have to do with performance and with substance. Substantive consideration is related to time only in that there is never enough of the latter for complete and permanent accomplishment. It is unfortunate when a board puts time limitations on the employment of the man or woman to whom they entrust the institution. When the chief administrator puts time limitations upon himself, he has missed the point of leadership and of responsibility. Responsibility cannot tolerate being confined or packaged or counted or timed. Leadership, as our colleges and schools, must be free. We cannot guarantee that freedom will always provide exemplary leadership, but the nature of man and of education demands that freedom must take its chances. For Americans and for all free people of the world the alternatives are too difficult to swallow and too impossible to digest.

Let us suppose that in spite of all of the foregoing to the contrary, our five-year man yields to the siren call of money or of prestige or of a long-considered magnetism toward another institution. What then? Another five- or ten-year plan, and then another? Who should be the judge at the end of each period? The Board, the Record, the Family, the Man himself? Five will get you ten that all of these entities will not vote the same way. And ten will get you twenty (or life) that much of the time our friend will experience uncomfortable and frustrating tugs back toward the school or college in which he had his first tastes of accomplishment or of disappointment.

The Groovy Life

Ponce de León was a perpetual searcher after the perpetually groovy life. With eternal youth would follow eternal health, enthusiasm, vigor, and idealism. While not entirely successful, Capitan de León has probably inspired some affirmative thinking about an impossible quest. Fortunately, he was an explorer in the true sense and not a school or college administrator, for then his search would have seemed all the more ludicrous. Where, may I ask in the most simple terminology possible, does one find the Fountain of Youth? Ponce could have found both the answer to his question and the end of his rainbow if only he had stumbled upon an elementary school or a small liberal arts college or a great university. He was, unfortunately, a few hundred years ahead of his time. But we are not. Yet, we continue to stumble along, trying to put measured human lives together to insure the immeasurable lives of our institutions. It is not an altogether groovy life, but it can be an exciting life-in-perpetuity. Is that not the primary plan and purpose of education?

It is an odd odyssey, this grasshopper journey looking for a mythical palace of perfection and a kingdom of comfort, stopping momentarily to slay a dragon or build a fortress or lay siege to a city, pausing long enough to make a positive contribution and to set an institution on a positive course, and then riding off in a new suit of armor (a suit of armor is not adequately broken in for twenty-five years or 250,000 miles, whichever occurs first) toward a challenge which seems greater and grander.

The constant looker wastes a good deal of physical, mental, and emotional energy in the looking process. If only that energy were to be harnessed and expended upon work *within* the institution and *for* those people who have put their futures into his hands. No need and no time to search afar for a better deal or a groovier life. A new life and a new experience are not always to be found elsewhere; a much better possibility exists when one stays at home. Ingenuity, excitement, ambition, drive, and enthusiasm can carry one just as far— perhaps farther—if he or she uses the advantages and the resources available at home and sparks them with a new determination to advance the same old institution with a new self.

There are ways for others to gauge visible progress of men and of schools, but there is only one way to measure the invisible growth and progress of a man's career, and that is by his own reflections. The only way for him to include an institution in this sort of measurement is to tie himself to it for a career's worth of time. The career principal or president is an exception, of course, particularly during the last decade or two. The rule has been to move rather than to stay. We know that some of these moves have been made for valid and justifiable reasons; we also know that a good number of them have been because of quasi-adventurous stirrings and a breathless urge to find *the* place. Long live the groovy life, and long live the realization that it can be found at home!

For the Good of the Institution

When a chief administrator begins rationalizing a decision to move which he has already made, his unimagination reaches heights previously unknown. One of the loftiest of these (one which most of his constituencies can accept without losing their hair and which the subsequently formed presidential search committee can confidently use on the prospective lineup of successors) is that the resignation was tendered "for the good of the institution." There is possibly no limit to the interpretations of a statement of this sort. It makes everyone a little more comfortable even though a thousand questions come to mind, including puzzlement over the *real* reason. This can be even more interesting when the move is made to a more affluent school district or to a more prestigious college with a larger endowment and several hundred thousands of dollars in operating reserves.

What is truly administratively good for an institution? We think immediately of stability and continuity of leadership. Someone to believe in its principles and purposes and destinies. Someone who will give of himself or herself to the sort of unique bond which can only exist between an institution and a man or woman who considers it to be alive and who fights to keep it healthy through good times and bad. We simply cannot develop significant arguments against these essentials. How, then, can we so quickly rationalize an action which is completely incompatible? The shock waves of separation and of breaking the bond do not affect the administrator alone. If such were so, he could be wished well and be encouraged to hope that his pain would rapidly diminish and that his new responsibilities would cauterize the wounds of alienation. But what of the institution and of its periodic reaction to leadership abandonment? We must still ask the meaning of "for the good of the institution" and wonder about *whose* good and *what* institution.

One Last Move

The fascination of considering one last position prior to planned or compulsory retirement has always fascinated me. What the chief administrator (or teacher or professor or minister or business executive) seems to be saying is that he or she would like one more adventure. Not one more chance or one more proof that he is needed or one more seat of power, but one more adventure. If this is true (and many individuals with whom I have talked say that it is) then why move? What it takes for one more adventure is a change of attitude, not a change of school or of community. One last burst of enthusiasm, one last affirmative motivation, one last positive administrative push —these are attitude centered, not location centered.

When a man or woman looks back on a twenty-five year career, especially if it has been spent in only one or two institutions, a quick look ahead lends a sense of urgency to the self-posed question, "Shouldn't I make one last move? I've only fifteen years left and the last twenty-five have gone by in a rush." Strong argument, but consider the home institution. Consider the college or school where that active and adventurous rush took place. Is there still room for enthusiasm, for motivation, for energy, for leadership forged in excitement and tempered by experience?

One last move, unless one's current position and responsibilities are irreconcilably intolerable, can more easily carry disappointment than satisfaction. It is, by definition and by declaration, the *last* move, which can bring negative pressures as well as positive opportunities. It can be a terminal avenue of no escape; a commitment which one would feel must be kept even though it might result in negative experience. Even if one is big enough to admit a mistake, it is quite another thing to live with it until retirement. The alternative is to make *another* last move. Psychologically, the syndrome affecting the one-last-move man is contrary to the attitude which has kept him in one place. There are exceptions, of course, but I suspect that decision of one last move for most is made against a background of long periods of service at one or two institutions.

Surely, there is important work to do without pulling up deep and established roots in order to make one last move. Consider one last thrust for education, for young people, and for mankind—doesn't this make more sense? From where can one thrust to greatest advantage? From where he or she already has feet firmly planted and where there is a cadre of proven and loyal colleagues to help.

When the Time Has Come

It cannot be denied that there are sometimes present conditions under which a chief administrator must move. It is my belief that many are manufactured, imagined, or grasped as reasons to justify a worthy or unworthy motive in changing jobs, but setting aside these unfortunate attitudinal misconceptions, we know that for some the time arrives when moving is the only answer. For reasons of health, finances, loss of self-confidence, loss of institutional confidence, irreparable error in judgment, and many more, a chief educational executive must be separated or must separate himself from the school or college or university he serves. It can be interpreted as a positive separation if it is self-imposed; it could be negative, personally and for the institution, if it is not.

There is sound argument for separation on the very simple basis that principal or president and school or college are incompatible. This does not necessarily indicate a professional failure or an institutional inflexibility. It most often means that the wrong connection has been made. If both the chief administrator and the institution clearly recognize the mistake, then separation is a totally affirmative and quiet procedure. In actual fact, the usual conditions are more complex and the process is very visible, very costly, and very damaging both within and without the institutional sphere. The school or college can weather the storm; too often, the person cannot. Disillusioned and deeply wounded, he is likely to move *out* instead of *on*.

The matter of attitude surfaces again. If one can convince himself that out of separation comes the opportunity for choice to find another field of interest or to take his skills and ideals to another set of institutional circumstances—then his chances for reasoned and wise decision are much enhanced. Even a separation and its subsequent moving on can be personally beneficial and institutionally sound. Let us admit, however, that the hard cases of incompatibility are rare and that far more often than not there is no mystery in moving on. Only myth.

XII. The Legend of Loneliness

On a scale of time, the single, lonely decision which must be made by the chief educational administrator is but momentary. The balance of administrative life should be filled with consultation, discussion, evaluation, and weighing of alternatives. Such action involves interaction, and interaction involves groups of people. If a principal or a president feels lonely in his room-at-the-top, it is more than likely his fault. One of the first steps toward loneliness is to withdraw from the action and, in so doing, to unconsciously discard professional and personal friendships along with problems.

If academic camaraderie is the prime objective for an institutional leader, he is, to be most generous, missing the point. To borrow and to tamper with a well known phrase, a leader is not supposed to win friends: he is supposed to influence people. Often, such influence can occur within an atmosphere of friendship, but it is a difficult task to mix friendship and influence. Excessive exercise in this direction can lead to loneliness. To reemphasize a point, however, such loneliness need only be momentary *unless the chief himself* wants or causes it to be permanent.

Allow, if you please, an illustration : In a situation which is charged with the electricity of a school or college-wide crisis, financial, academic, social, or whatever, the necessity for wide sharing of opinion for options leading to final decision is obvious. That final decision cannot be made under any consideration of "friends" won or lost. When the crisis is over and business as usual (or unusual) has been restored, the president or principal still stands ready to make the next decision alone, but he does not have to stand *apart*. The institution has received his primary consideration and the people within it, even though some are disappointed or angry, can understand his position more readily than if he had politicized the decision in terms of counting friends.

Relationships with various institutional constituencies must be established on the basis of confidence and trust, on the basis of friendship. Students, faculty, and administrative colleagues have a unique relationship to the chief executive. Friendship of this sort must transcend the sometimes heated discussion and the occasional compromise or the independently firm position taken by the chief executive. The responsibility for maintaining friendships at a professionally worthy and personally satisfying level is, after all, up to the person in final authority. If presidential-constituent relationships were truly two-way streets, many a discouraging confrontation would be avoided, but the highest office demands the highest essentials of leadership, and this includes putting decisions before friendships. If such actions lose "friends," then one must reluctantly accept the fact.

When an administrative chief indulges in self-pity, and when he sees imaginary problems and ghost enemies, and when he dwells upon those responsibilities which he must face alone, then he can drive himself into a singular, sedentary administration. This is unfortunate, not only for him but for those who could be close to him most of the time and for the school or college which has selected him for his potential qualities of leadership. As previously noted or implied, administration is an active occupation; *to lead* is an active verb, more readily an interactive verb. One cannot interactively lead in self-resigned solitary confinement.

Out on a Limb

When a president or principal discovers that he or she is making a good number of decisions reflecting a distinct minority, even when such are preceded by broad counsel, it may well be time to look inward and to ponder if one is (pick your own metaphor) : out on a limb, out in left field, or paddleless or canoeless up a creek. There is a wonderful Berryman political cartoon involving the late, great Senator William Borah of Idaho which more graphically illustrates the point. Pictured as a drum major, Senator Borah is enthusiastically high-stepping his way down the road to continued isolationism, while his brass band and the rest of the parade have turned the corner toward world involvement. There may be a dual illustration here for those who need it. Leading a lonely parade away from involvement, even if you are right, would seem to indicate the unfortunate combination of "I want to be alone" and "Where did everybody go?" Regardless, being too far from the center of things or being too *far out* for one's following constituencies can be the beginning of a sort of loneliness that is difficult to mend, friendship or understanding notwithstanding. Some would counter with the possibility that perhaps the view is better when one is up in a tree, especially on that side of the tree where the limb he is out on is located. But a high view of possible disaster strikes me as a strange way to improve perspective. And everyone knows what happens "when the bough breaks."

One's colleagues cannot give him support unless they know when or how he needs it. The isolationist administrator complains of his lonely existence, yet will not reach out for help or for counsel or even for company. "Don't get too near the troops" is another of those ancient rationalizations for self-imposed loneliness. Once again, we have forgotten that we have ultimate responsibility for the troops and if we are always out on a limb, even a friendly and familiar one, we cannot exercise that responsibility to its deserved or required degree. Responsibility implies a personal closeness; closeness defies loneliness. A very practical and sensible way to get off the dangerous end of any limb, it seems to me, is to reach out for and accept the help of those for whom one has responsibility and with whom one can find warmth and understanding. Not universal agreement, not total compatibility, not always majority in agreement or consensus, but certainly warmth and understanding. The leader who must sometimes make lonely decisions need not be a perennial alien in his own land unless it is his own wish to be so.

Off on a Tangent

"Where is the president?"
"Off on another tangent."
Off raising money, off recruiting faculty, off at national meetings, off on a speaking engagement, perhaps just "off." One or two of these

are understandable by the academic community even if the remainder are not completely palatable. But "off on a tangent" has ominous overtones of flirting with unreality and of accompanying invitations to loneliness. The specific tangents and their possible uselessness to the contrary, the general reaction to a presidential or principalian suggestion for marked departure from "the way we have always done things" is cautious, to say the very least. To say the very most would not only be inappropriate, but very probably unprintable. The institutional reaction to chief administrative tangents is quite predictable. It would seem that any presidential objective, no matter how tangential or reasonable, requires time and patience and friendly ears.

What seems to be an absolutely unthinkable, unspeakable, unworkable proposal from the principal's or president's office in, say, early February, can become a logical, promising masterpiece of thought for the institution coming out of an ad hoc study committee in late April. In the interim, who is lonely? No one. The chief administrative officer is off on another tangent; the faculty is reacting to and wrestling with the last one; most of the students are in the library; and the chairman of the board is pleased that everyone is busy. Positive or negative tangents simply cannot be properly identified until they have been discussed and evaluated and then adopted or discarded. For that matter, how many "tangents" discarded in 1950 would be unanimously adopted in 1973? The interesting thing, I think, is that what usually starts out as a tangent ends up being "the way we have always done things." If the process makes a temporarily lonely figure of the chief administrator, then it is worth the discomfort. Institutional rigor mortis is to be avoided. Rigor tangentialis can be one of the most promising signs of life.

Under the Desk

How can a man or woman hide and then complain of being lonely? Perhaps one of the basic inconsistencies of human beings, more visibly evidenced in positions of leadership, is to withdraw purposely from the action and then to publicly air grievance to the fact that his or hers is the loneliest job in the world.

One of our favorite phrases in welcoming new members to the faculty and staff (usually made in the presence of continuing members) is the routine which begins, "I want you to know that the door to my office is always open." This of course, is not true, and even if it were, it implies that the office occupant will always be there. Moreover, now that students and presidents or principals are saying more to each other these days, the routine can be altered only slightly and we have, "Drop by the office when you have a minute and let's talk about it." These are straightforward, honest, and forthright invitations from the chief executive of the institution to be commended and encouraged. But when they are accepted, as we hope they would be, and the invitee finds the president or principal is "out" or "in an important meeting," not once or twice but most of the time, then he stops trying. He also begins to wonder about other statements made by the chief. What eventually evolves is a sort of Open-Door Empty-Office policy. The administrator himself has strangled the opportunity which he created. When people stop coming to see him, the president gets lonesome. When the principal is totally unavailable, he gives up the chance to exercise his counsel with those who may critically need it.

It is perhaps unfair to indict an empty office or a closed door without again considering its positive aspects. As we have seen, there are reasons enough for an occasional hermitage and for the infrequent physical disappearance per the Cheshire Cat (if one remembers not to grin and thus to give oneself away). Occasional disappearance and being alone is necessary and even essential, not only in the midst of daily routine but during moments of major decision. Being alone, however, is not the same as being lonely. One affords the chance for putting things back into perspective, for creative thought, for catching one's breath; the other is often filled with anxiety, frustration, self-doubt, and misery. Whether a person is lonely or alone depends, in great measure, *upon him* rather than upon his surroundings and his colleagues. It depends upon whether he views his basic responsibility to the institution as human-oriented rather than corporation-oriented.

Monophobia, the fear of being alone, can be a cancerous phenomenon which can take over the entire possession of thought and action.

The best place to hide is "under the desk." But when most of one's time is spent beneath the big mahogany box which represents the center of institutional influence, then being alone and fearing to be alone play a continuing and growing game which feeds upon the unknowing and unfortunate victim. How can a proud, self-assured, enthusiastic, and energetic new president, principal, or superintendent wake up one day to find himself under the desk : cut off from the mainstream of his institution, rejected by his colleagues, alienated from the challenges and opportunities which he actively sought and solidly faced ? He has *separated himself* from the essence of the position he holds. He has defaulted from participation in the current life of the institution and from active projection and planning for its future. How much can he do and how far can he see, under the desk ?

Over the Rainbow

A scarecrow in need of a brain. A tin man in need of a heart. A tired and beleaguered lion in need of courage. One could easily have the feeling that the Kingdom of Academia is located in the Land of Oz and that the yellow brick road is permanently closed. It would seem to be much easier to resign oneself to sitting calmly and drowsily in a field of poppies and, unresisting, to allow the winged monkeys to carry one away. But however persistently real is the need for brain, heart, and courage and however continuingly real the problems in Academia, there is no room for the make-believe of somnifacient poppy fields, winged monkeys, and the recurring wish that the job can be done alone. Presidents have been called worse than brainless, heartless, and cowardly (at least one has been) and so, I suspect, have principals and superintendents. One can be called many things without effect other than personal ; what one *is* can be critical to interpersonal relationships and to career. Neither need have anything to do with loneliness.

Over the rainbow toward those solitary expeditions, the results of which can only be shared with one's closest colleagues and advisers, if at all, can create false impressions of secrecy within the heart and brain of the institution ; within the minds of those wonderful yet, by nature, inquisitive people who teach and learn and are the very center of the life of the institution. There are times when the chief administrator can translate and explain the reasons for a necessary trip to Oz and report on the favorable or unfavorable outcome of such a journey. There are times when he or she must communicate with the total enterprise about independent actions which are going on and which may have great effect upon it, even though such communication can but carry the message that it is impossible to go into detail until a later time. Again we see an opportunity for constituent confidence rather than for an invitation to loneliness.

If a chief executive officer reflects mystery, or even more dangerously, goes out of his way to create it, reactions of those about him will be completely and appropriately predictable : "What's going on? Why isn't he telling us about it?" Brains, hearts, and courage are precious characteristics, both in personal and institutional terms. For a principal, president, or superintendent to assume he has a corner on the supply is unthinkable; for his colleagues and constituents to believe that he seems to be periodically disappearing over the rainbow to sharpen and replenish his own supply is not too far from truth. A return at reasonable intervals and a briefing on as much as circumstances will allow is reassuring to nearly everyone.

On the Inside

To be truly inside, a president or principal must not act like an outsider. He can never again be "one of the gang." He gives up that special relationship when he accepts the top administrative position, but he can be closely involved with the gang in those activities and explorations and concerns which always dominate the total institution. In this regard, then, both he and his colleagues are a part of a larger consideration. This concept, together with arguments previously submitted, leads me to call for the complete refutation of the legend which perpetuates the idea of "none but the lonely president."

If we allow ourselves to think of presidential or principalian "power" or influence as being at the *center* rather than at the *top,* then perhaps this entire concept of loneliness *vs.* involvement can be made more clear. When power or influence moves down from the top, it often leaves the chief administrator in a position of isolation or detachment. His grasp on the vehicle which carries the downward force can be lost and his grasp of its effects upon others during the filtering-down process can become proportionately less with distance.

Contrast this action with influence which emanates from the *center*. The movement will perhaps be slower when starting at the center because it must move against a concentric continuum of resistance rather than against a single point, the apex of a triangle. It is my firm belief that this concentric pressure is better for all concerned. Moreover, if begun at the center, the internal movement of force behind a proposal or an idea is theoretically equal until it reaches the outermost confines of the institutional entity. Central detection of reaction is more readily determined than that which must work its way back up through a hierarchical monolith. It can be lonely at the top; it is anything but lonely at the center.

Developments within the 1950's and 1960's have made it easier for the chief administrator to be with and to talk with students, faculty, and the various other constituencies. What were first thought to be roads to institutional ruin and the creation of irreparably wide schisms within a school, college, or university have proven, with time, to be completely new levels of common concern. It is unfortunately true that in the white-hot forge of misunderstanding, inflexibility, and violence which devastated some campuses and relationships, common concerns were lost in the name of cause or insurrection. But as is so often the case, and as history keeps doggedly reminding us, the many learned some lessons from the few. As a result, we are making real progress toward the discovery or rediscovery of our institutional purposes and identities. This has taken joint identification, joint evaluation, and a joint resolution with all segments of the institution in mind. The chief executive appropriately spends more and more of his time at the center and reserves his traditional place at the top for the sorts of pragmatic decisions which are becoming less and less frequent. Loneliness has become, for most of us, a forgotten relic. Some of us are predicting that even the legend will not last.

XIII. Wide-Angle Lensmanship

ONE OF THE MOST DIFFICULT yet most necessary positions for a chief administrator to take goes something like this: "The course of action we will follow is one which I consider to be appropriate for the total institution; it is, I feel, in the best interests of the most concerned." However debatable by however many, the administrator in authority is the only one who can finally take such a position, and his is the only position which can be interpreted as speaking for the entire school, college, or system. Even as this is so, it is also well to remember that his is the final decisional responsibility and thus he is to be held fully responsible. His skill in mustering individual strengths to total strength is one of the keys to the vault which holds answers to such considerations. His broad view and his concept of the totality of institutional action and reaction must be one of the primary bases for schoolwide policy.

Many teachers, students, board members, and administrative people should and do periodically stand back and survey the goals and the progress of an institution. This is usually done, as we all know, informally, continually, and subconsciously. All are searching for ways to improve their own individual units and areas, and in so doing, to improve the school or college or university. Occasionally, surveying is done in a formal and organized manner, not only through established or ad hoc committees but by the periodic scheduling of special programs of discussion and recommendation which bring representatives of the various constituencies of the institution together for creative and self-educating conversation. (Completely apart from the foregoing is the preaccreditation exercise which can have positive wide-angle viewing possibilities.) The principal or president should initiate such programs or, if the suggestions and requests for such come from others, should be ready to endorse and sponsor them. However, his or her charge goes far beyond initiation

117

of and participation in joint evaluation, because he or she is uniquely related to the institution and, thus, to its evaluation. Because he or she is not only responsible for overall judgment but also responsible for its manifestation. Thus one man or woman can materially control the attitude and the urgency of schoolwide evaluation; he or she can make or break both the strength and continuity of the measurement of the institution.

In a continuing institutional evaluative role, the chief administrator must not, it seems to me, allow detail to interfere with sweep. A broad picture can often give a better sense of what is happening *totally,* just as a study in broad strokes of color and pattern is more conceptually complete than the narrow and definitive line detail of sharp and clinical black and white. Gauguin's suggestions and hints and subtle nuances of light and color capture entire island landscapes. In order to capture sand granules, hermit crab tracks, and rockweed spores, one must zoom inside the reef, over the tide pools, and up onto a very narrow sliver of beach. I will concede that this sort of microscopic scrutiny is ultimately essential after the broad decision for restructuring curriculum or revising the tenure regulations has been made, but first must come the search for liberal scope and wide-angle vista which can give the chief executive his best assessment of total pattern and total growth potential or afford him the opportunity to place narrow and scattered considerations into appropriate wide-angle perspective.

Perspective involves not only width, but also length: focal length. One need only remember his or her first efforts in getting a family group photograph into satisfactory focal proportion. Too close, and noses were as dominant as a tapir's and both grandma and Uncle Ed disappeared. Too far away, and subjects become not only noseless but faceless as well and Uncle Ed was indistinguishable from Aunt Grace. Fortunately (or unfortunately) for posterity, grandma always identified the group and the occasion by writing on the back of each print: family, Christmas, 1947, or whatever. Where can one stand for optimum wide-angle and precise focal observation? Here is where we must admit that just as all cameras have their individual idiosyncrasies, so do chief administrators have critical differences in their own definitions and practices of the range and dimension which seems best for them. A modern, wide-angle lens will help; an old-fashioned, wide-angle attitude is essential.

On the Retina of the Beholder

Seeing is variously described and variously interpreted. An image, interestingly upside down, on the retina of the eye is recorded as such in terms of a pure, physical phenomenon. It takes an optic nerve and an accompanying round-trip message to the brain to turn it right-side up, and it takes some degree of previous experience for recognition. The image only appears on the retina of the beholder, and it takes more than an image to make comparisons, to reach conclusions, and to make choices. Seeing has also acquired implications of understanding. Understanding, too, is dependent upon more or less intelligence and upon more or less experience with things identical or similar. "I see" is not always "I understand."

We know from experimentation that eyes and optic nerves and brains can seem to lie to us. We know that two people "see" the same things in an entirely different manner, physiologically as well as psychologically. If we rely upon the use of different or additional lenses or upon a variety of light filters, we can alter the conditions of the image seen and of the understanding "seen." And, although combinations of optical lenses and filters afford an opportunity to see over fences, through clouds, and around corners, no one has yet developed a way for a principal or a president to make cogent administrative use of such devices. The wider, higher, and more deeply he can see are of real help; but seeing in the abstract has no philosophical relationship to periscopes, microscopes, spectroscopes, or telescopes. Kaleidoscopes, perhaps, but even though kaleidoscopic designs and patterns change, the impact on the whole of the circle is disappointingly similar after the first few turns. Ten minutes, and the observer can quickly become preoccupied with extended differences in similarity.

Making use of wide-angle vision in order to take the sorts of actions that affect a wide segment, if not the entire corpus, of an

institution is the more difficult second step. One can view situations
from near and far, collect and catalog impressions, even devise and
put into readiness a wide-angle plan to match a current need and
beyond. Action, however, is where many of us fall short of requisite
responsibility.

If I may again be repetitive, for no other reason than for the sake
of my own understanding and clarification, it seems to me that wide-
angle vision and wide-angle planning are of no value whatsoever if
they are not followed by wide-angle action. This cannot mean action
to include the wishes of everyone; it can mean action that is all-inclu-
sive in its effect and action which must be taken with the feelings
and futures of the greatest number in mind. In some rare instance,
it can even mean taking an action which a large majority of the people
of an institution do not think they want and in a purely democratic
situation would vote against. Action of this sort reflects those infrequent occasions when an institution must assume the characteristics of a near-monarchy. A benevolent "monarch" can usually
emerge bloodless under such conditions if they are rare, and if the
final result is a happy one. Unfortunately, the decision for action cannot count upon either happy results or upon satisfied constituents.
Underlining once more, let us always remember that we were selected
and appointed *to take actions* regardless of personal risk. We are
vulnerable daily and hourly, and though we learn to live with the
delicate balance of responsibility, it cannot be allowed to tip one way
or the other for personal or political reasons.

Convex or Concave?

The picture of life in any of our educational institutions should
never be described as flat. Mirrored by our people, our programs,
and our own specific and unique character, we cannot afford to be,
or to be seen, in terms of a straight line or a single surface. Yet this
reflection is far more common than we realize or than we should
tolerate.

What are some alternatives? One, at least, is deliberate distortion.
An oblique reviewing angle, for example, gives one an opportunity

for new measurement and new perspective. Human images, viewed from the front row, side, at the Bijou seem taller than life. They go through the same sorts of experiences and, although additional concentration on the part of the viewer is required, they simply move at odd angles and with distorted actions that our eyes have difficulty in accommodating. Any help in evaluation? I think so. Because a continuous view from twentieth row orchestra can lead our eyes and brains down a misleading pathway. An occasional look from a different angle can point the way toward reassurance that achievements and failures are not confined to a single view.

Another consideration of deliberate distortion is the use of aberrational reflection. This involves another sort of purposeful imperfect vision which alters the exact point-to-point image. This seems appropriate, for no person, no institution, no concept of education is without flaw. We live in imperfection and, as such, it reflects imperfectly upon ourselves and those around us. The lesson is in learning to *see* the way we are and to *see* the way we want to be. In the ultimate of reflective aberration, we can take a brief journey into the Hall of Mirrors. I am thinking here of that hall of mirrors to be found in the Fun House rather than in the Palace at Versailles. Natural bulges in unnatural places or vice versa can be unrealistically mirrored in those long and undulating looking glasses which, I have thought at times, were designed by a student-faculty committee so that we administrators could see ourselves as others see us. From nose to toes, our imperfections are bigger than life but true to form: tiny heads, permanently clenched fists, weak eyes, no ears, rusty pocketbooks, and warped dispositions.

The first objective look can be shattering to both individual and to mirror. A long look in either convex or concave dimension is good for an institution. Imperfections are exaggerated to the point that they become instantly obvious. Not so in a conventional mirror, especially one in which the chief viewer has been making optical and psychological corrections for so long that he ignores the lumps and bumps and ruts and grooves which ought to be corrected by action rather than by lens makers or dream makers.

View of Point

One of the things we so often forget is that institutions, like the time which ultimately governs them, are on an endless journey. This means a constantly changing landscape with a permanent life and a constantly changing cast of characters with measurable and terminal lives. Those of us who assume the role of chief reviewer, evaluator, and wide-angle lensman need a *view of point* much more than we need a point of view. It cannot be stationary, a lookout tower, a lighthouse, or a high rimrock, because if it is the institution we view and the parade we watch will pass us by. We need to move with the total pattern, be a part of it, and yet, at the same time, be detached. Our view of point cannot always be of three hundred and sixty degrees. It cannot take into consideration that others may be able to view us more clearly than we view ourselves. A view of point, the point of what we are trying to do and what our institutions must do to stay awake and alive, is the view with which only one set of eyes per institution can be charged at a time. What is the point of it all and why is it important to see the Point of it all?

√ The Point means more than location. It means more than district or school or college. It means more than campus. It means more than attitudes and goals and accomplishments.

√ The Point means a reason for continuing existence. It must be justified every day of the year and every year into numberless years ahead.

√ The Point is the reason why our system of education has endured generation after generation of criticism, witch-hunting, misunderstanding, and ridicule, and why it has again and again survived such threats to remain vigorous and healthy and defiant. Its adaptability, its innate tensile strength, its stubborn ability to always bounce back—these are some of the supportive reasons for The Point.

√ The Point also means a person. A person who must also stand and fight for what he believes. A person who believes in and who understands that periodic change is necessary for personal sanity and for institutional survival. If he has this *view of point,* or *points,* then a wide-angle attitudinal view can be of help to him. If not, then a widened view of nothing is as useless as it sounds.

While negative points of view are all too common, it has always seemed to me impossible to have a completely negative *view of point*. One can certainly view the negative aspects of an imperfect institution and of an imperfect self, but sight and insight can be positive enough and objective enough to see not only imperfections but to attempt to do something about them. One cannot have a completely negative *view of point* and remain in a role of leadership. Because the point of it all is worth the sacrifice and the challenge and the alternate moments of despair and exaltation characterizing the wonderful and critically important work which we have undertaken and which we have made an inseparable part of ourselves and of our professional lives.

Just One More, Please—and Smile

Alfred Stieglitz did not take passport photos. This late nineteenth and early twentieth century photographic artist was never satisfied with the results of his work. He was always searching for new techniques, new concepts, new ways to make his exquisite craftsmanship totally acceptable as one of the fine arts. That he succeeded is, of course, an historic and aesthetic reality. Stieglitz and his superb creations went a step further than that of giving photography its rightful place among the arts. His influence upon painters and printmakers such as Georgia O'Keefe and Edward Hopper extended the patterns and contrasts and impressions of his photographs into surrounding media. Not only were he and his art accepted by a previously doubting community, they became the fecund nucleus for a revolution in all of American art.

It is interesting to contemplate the result of a Stieglitz street scene or cityscape if, in his time, he had been given benefit of later photographic technology, including light filters, automatic range finders, and the wide-angle lens. Yet we know that Stieglitz, as any creative genius, probably had need of little else than the basic material with which to work. PATIENCE, in order to wait for that precise moment when the natural light was within the possibility of the ultimate. UNDERSTANDING, in order to breathe exciting life into a common image and, in turn, to take life from it. BELIEF IN SELF and in cause, in order to practice a craft or an art with confidence and to be unencumbered by the consuming demons of anxiety and doubt. MOTIVATION, in order to continue to search for perfection, knowing it can never be found in the mind or heart of the searcher. CREATIVITY, in order to satisfy the basic need in all intelligent and sensitive human beings to accomplish a unique piece of work. PERSUASION, in order to marshal all the rest into a reasonable and useful whole and then to lead it somewhere. These were the real tools of Alfred Stieglitz. They were instruments of the spirit and of the soul: extensions of influence and of perception and of concern. Stieglitz had no need of a wide-angle lens. He had a wide-angle view of life and of his place in it.

What are the wide-angle tools of a superintendent or a principal or a president or a trustee? Patience, understanding, belief in self and cause, motivation, creativity, and persuasion.

Stand right over there—a little closer—now, just one more please, and smile.

XIV. To Defend the Tower

EDUCATION NEEDS SUPPORT from every corner of society. Certainly, support is required from those who have chosen a career in education, especially from leaders and would-be leaders in chief administrative posts. Support sometimes means defense. Running off "in quest of new truth and new purpose" is to be admired and encouraged, yet under some circumstances is not as important to total leadership as to stand and defend what is already believed to be true and purposeful. The only professional employe of an educational institution who can defend it with a voice of authority is its chief executive.

More often than one would like to contemplate, close institutional constituents seem to behave as if they feel that putting the institution down deserves more of their time and energy than building it up. Dwelling on the negative in some instances becomes the favorite indoor and outdoor sport of educators. Perhaps there is an element of human nature at work here—constant criticism of an organ which is known to be imperfect is, in the eyes of some, justified. "Make it better by finding fault with it" is a curious twist of corrective character, a strange upside down and backward frame of mind which often defeats its own purpose.

It is one thing to look regularly and realistically at a school, college, or university in terms of its present imperfect position and in terms of its flaws and its unfulfilled potentials and its broken promises. It is quite another to become so deeply involved in criticism that there is no time left for corrective action. To isolate negative elements and to engage in endless and fruitless conversation about them is perhaps great entertainment in faculty lounges, dormitory rooms, trustee committee sessions, and chief administrative discussion groups at national meetings. But identification and illumination of problems cannot, by themselves, accomplish change or betterment. They are

125

only first steps. Another first step, and in another direction, is to begin with positive elements and to build upon them.

The Tower, still believed by some to be a fortress of intellect, has always been under attack. The relatively monastic life of those engaged in the giving or receiving of "an education" has been alternately respected and despised, revered and suspected, sought after and ignored or purged. The most recent attacks have come from all quarters and for a variety of reasons. Many segments of a once respectful public are now beating on the doors, not to get in but to knock them down, as if destruction of walls and of practices and of concepts will somehow slow or divert the ongoing human appetite for intellectual advancement.

The idea that a young man or woman can temporarily dwell within the protective walls of the tower while strengthening and polishing his or her intellect or while preparing for a wider, more abundant life has now somehow acquired a sort of national resentment. Moreover, the idea that a teacher or a professor or an administrator can permanently reside in such an atmosphere has further nurtured the traditional belief that "those people" are different. Of course, there is no tower; no one has really ever lived there; there is and always has been a "real world" of education. If we are not in the position of defending the tower, the moat, the drawbridge, and the monastic life, what, then? We are defending the purposes and principles of education. Improving, growing, strengthening, taking steps and making strides toward meeting a continuous stream of demands and responsibilities. Tradition and innovation *at the same time*.

The Anti Syndrome

The plus or minus condition of anything is affected by the description of it. Those who talk about any entity in negative terms, even though there are varying degrees of truth in what they say, are furthering the negative aspects of such an entity. Because of the extremely high visibility of education (everyone is an expert, including most of the "experts"), it is especially vulnerable to the anti syndrome or the Academian flu virus. Those who too diligently concentrate on weak spots can further weaken an institution by

ignoring strengths on which to build. How often we see an accumulative negative effect; how seldom the opposite. But let us look
at the building process in light of these two alternatives—two alternatives because a third or neutral position is important only as a
transitional attitude on the way up.

We usually think of going on the defensive when a negative
position or condition exists. It is easier to defend a positive position.
And it is easier to build an accumulative positive condition. If we
spend our constant energies and our total concentrations upon weaknesses, we leave to chance the further development of strengths.
Strengths have carried schools and colleges through the cyclical
nature of their emotional, economic, and philosophical existences.
Strengths are to be won, and lost, and won again. *Strengths* and
their building and defense deserve more than a secondary consideration by any institution and by its chosen officer in authority.

If we could bring Sir Isaac Newton into the conversation, I think
he would remind us, even under transfer into the abstract, that a
"body in motion tends to stay in motion." A Newtonian momentum
of positive institutional attitude and of affirmative institutional
strength gives reason for the strong continuation of moment after
moment after moment. The surest psychological treatment for the
"anti syndrome" is positive involvement. The most effective remedy
for Academian flu virus is a giant inoculation of work toward the
building and sustaining of a positive and strengthening attitude;
institutions can have attitudes as well as people. The institutional
attitude of a school or college is greater or smaller than the sum
of the individuals within it. The president or principal reflects this
plus or minus attitude. Seeing to it that involvement, attitude, and
work are accumulatively positive is another of the direct responsibilities of the chief administrative officer.

Please Don't Apologize

When schools or school people are accused of making mistakes
or when inside or outside constituents are aware of a potential or
accomplished error, it is presidential or principalian authority which
must decide whether or not to verbalize the position of the institu-

tion. An automatic apology simply gives undue importance and perhaps false credence to a situation which may, as time and explanation clears up misunderstanding, require an apology from the accuser. The decision to reveal privately or publicly an institutional position during controversy is a tall order for one person, yet it is finally his to make. If we take three words or phrases that are usually involved in the process of answering criticisms from concerned constituents or antagonists, we may be able to clarify their differences and similarities and also shed some light on choice.

To ADMIT ERROR if, indeed, error has been committed, is a mark of courage. To admit error for the sake of an expedient "out" in a persistently uncomfortable relationship is a mark of cowardice. All too often, the admission of error, real or imagined, is followed by a lengthy and silent period of peace, or what seems to be a period of peace. There are questions to be asked in either case. If the error was real, has admission been followed by a conscious effort to correct the situation which prompted it? If it was not an error, has the possibility for future communication deteriorated because of the compromising of a belief which should have been fought for rather than surrendered? For a chief administrative officer to admit or to deny institutional error places heavy singular responsibility and he must be absolutely sure of his ground in order to accept that responsibility.

To DEFEND carries semantic implications that even though an error might have been made, there will be no admission—only the protection of a rigid position taken. We sometimes go to ridiculous extremes, you know, in order to defend those actions which everyone about us is certain are ill-fated even as they were ill-conceived. To defend blindly a weakened or dying institutional decision or personal mistake should be legally punishable. Such defense defies the essence of educational principle; it makes a mockery of the academic statesmanship and professionalism of which we are so valiantly trying to convince our friends, colleagues, and critics.

To APOLOGIZE can carry still another meaning. Apology should be reserved for a personal mistake or misdeed which adversely affects another person or persons or their lives. Institutions cannot apologize. Yet we use and over-use the apology as if it were required in every difficult situation involving institutional-constituent relationships. There is much loud talk of accountability these days (for the benefit of newcomers, there has always been talk of accountability) and several segments of society want to hold schools and colleges accountable. This is as impossible as an institution being held to an apology. *Persons* apologize to each other or for each other; institutions cannot.

What are my points in regard to apology, defense, and admission of error?

√ First, that admission of error is appropriate and healthy, *if* an error has been made. Criticism by a constituent does not automatically mean that an error has been made.

√ Second, that defense is appropriate and healthy, *if* that defense is not blind and is not conditioned by reflex action.

√ Third, that institutional apology is impossible and that personal apology is rarely called for. When, as chief administrative officers, we *speak for the institution* we serve, it is advisable and essential under certain circumstances, to admit error and to stand in defense. But please, let us not apologize.

Students Under Fire

During the past several years, the majority of the public has been grossly unfair to students. I am speaking in generalities here, in terms of the "public" as well as in terms of "the student." Focus has been on secondary school and college students, yet somewhat reflected upon all. The outside constituency, as well as much of the inside, has forgotten or has chosen to overlook the fact that most students are, and have been, and will always be difficult to fit into a mold in areas of communication, understanding, and reason. But we also overlook that it is *our* communication, *our* understanding, and *our* reason that we deem to be correct. An essential part of our culture involves young people growing to maturity and others watching them do it. This is uncomfortable, though necessary, for both the watched and the watching. In education, we are more deeply involved because we cannot sit and watch. We must involve ourselves in the process, often to a greater degree than parents. Young people are active, sensitive, growing, reaching organisms. These days they are saying and doing many courageous things, many of the things that the rest of us have long wanted to say or to do. Why are we not applauding rather than booing? They live in a world of their own in addition to the one we all live in. Have we taken the time to listen and to look?

As we battle over what we think is best for students, they are too often lost in the smoke and the noise. Whether a student takes his education actively or passively, he learns. He learns by wandering off the pathway once in a while. He learns by making a mistake or by having something turn out satisfactorily. He learns from the experiences and the knowledge of others. He learns from himself. All this *in spite of* our discussions and arguments and entanglements over what is best for him. When things go wrong, the student is under fire. How can we go on defending the tower and leave the student vulnerable to criticisms which basically reflect our shortcomings, not his?

Students should not, except under certain conditions, be anything but students. They are in the tower to prepare for their futures, and this principally means to learn. They cannot hold the corporate charter; they cannot teach; they cannot directly govern; they cannot invest or sell institutional assets. But have we given them enough latitude *as students*? Have we given them enough room to breathe and grow and reach? Have we considered them *first* in matters of teaching and learning? Have we given them freedom to make both individual successes and individual mistakes? Have we defended their right to be wrong?

Banners vs. Placards

Perhaps we have forgotten how to carry banners. Banners were once a symbol of pride and of camaraderie; a rallying point and a tangible evidence of something in which to believe. Some of today's banners are placards. Placards are a symbol of protest, sometimes peaceful, sometimes hostile, but always of protest. They can also reflect pride and also something in which to believe. Are banners and placards so different? Does a comparison boil down to pride *vs.* protest, or are there elements of both in each? No matter how we who are on the firing line differentiate or parallel these symbols of the old and the new, those on the periphery usually associate banners with ancient and time-honored right, and they categorize protest, placards, and disruptive behavior as wrong. Banners proclaim "Hooray for something!" Placards are scrawled with "Down with everything!" Can we look at this seeming difference of opinion in another way and better arrive at some sort of answer?

Suppose that the messages and the conveyances were reversed. Suppose that cardboard placards, hurriedly nailed to sticks, were emblazoned with the proud crest of the educational explorer and that purple velvet banners were embroidered with bold and golden letters which spelled out "Meet Our Demands, or Else!" Which of their respective carriers and followers would be marching proudly with righteous educational zeal? Which would be brazenly picketing, disturbing the educational peace, and creating a "bad image" for Academia? Banners *vs.* placards is not the issue. Pride *vs.* protest is not the issue. Remaining, then, is to recognize that what counts is the way we carry our symbols and the way which we attain what they purportedly stand for.

Those who choose either the quiet way or the noisy way can be equally defended. A banner carrier has no less pride than a placard holder; there have been traditional standard bearers throughout history who had a great deal more to protest than those who carry signs on sticks. *Belief* in cause and seriousness of purpose do not ally themselves to either gold leaf or poster paint. We must pay attention to both banners and placards because both have much to say. Some of it is not related to principle; some of it is noisy for the sake of making noise or quiet for the effect that quietness can have, but a good portion of it is serious and courageous and its implementation can lead to an improvement of the status quo.

Banners can be trampled and placards cast aside in retreat or
defeat. I would prefer to see both carried forward with purpose *and*
with pride. If we believe in our young people and in our chosen
careers to live and work among them, then we are wasting our time
in defending either banners or placards. We should be defending the
ideas, the probings, the possibilities, the discontent with mediocrity,
and the right to climb which both banner and placard proclaim.

Proud and Abandoned: A Parable

Once a proud and prosperous people lived in a valley which was
protected by the mountains, by the sea, and by a great wall which
was built across a narrow inlet, the only natural means of access.
Atop the wall stood a tower which afforded a view of the valley
and of the threat of invasion by hostile forces. Soldiers patrolled
the mountain passes and the beaches and stood guard behind the
parapets of the great wall. For several hundreds of years circumstances were kind and, though vigilant, the defenders of the people
and of the tower were not challenged to fight for the preservation
of the life they enjoyed. Bountiful crops and vintage years allowed
great stores of grain and of wine to be stored against the possibility
of battle or famine. A time of peace and plenty with the power
necessary for protection. Few kingdoms could boast such a fortunate
condition.

The tower was at the center of the life of the people. It was the
symbol of their strength and of their heritage. Even though some
future and unimaginable enemy might thunder down upon the valley
from the mountains or storm the inlet from the sea or scale the
great wall, the tower was large enough to hold them all and strong
enough to protect them all. They became a kingdom unto themselves
with no need to venture from their valley; no need for trade or for
exchange of goods or news or ideas.

One day in late summer, tower lookouts espied two winding and
endless columns of enemy soldiers advancing along the shore and
the ridge of the mountain. On and on they came, closer to the valley
and the great wall and the proud tower. The people of the kingdom

made ready for battle. They doubled their defenses and mustered their troops and moved their weaponry into position. Those who were left took refuge in the tower. At last, they were to be put to the test. Pride and power surged through the heart of the land and echoed throughout the tower. Then the invaders stopped. Encircling the valley, they camped on the beaches and in the foothills. Days and weeks and months of siege followed. At first, no discomfort was felt, only frustration. The tower granaries and cellars, once bulging with sustenance, began to run alarmingly low. Attempts at forage in the once-fertile valley or upon the channel to the sea, were met with disaster.

Pride would carry them through, thought leaders and wise men. Pride of the Ancients, their ancestors, and precursors. Pride in achievement, in symbol, and in legend. Pride did not sour with the last of the wine. Spirit did not break with the final ration of grain. Pride was strong and defiant until the end.

There was no conquest, no occupation, no victorious entry. The enemy, as so often happens, had no predetermined design for expanding territory or extending boundary. They had neither the motivation nor the knowledge to recreate the pleasant kingdom of before. They had proven their superiority. They withdrew as they had come. The tower was empty; an abandoned derelict symbol of pride. Wind and dust became its ageless companions, and no one ever bothered to defend it again.

XV. Challenges and Rewards

NOT ALL CHALLENGES are met with reward; not all rewards are immediately evident. A principal, a superintendent, a president, provost, or chancellor does not accept a position of highest responsibility in education with reward in mind. Ours is a career and a profession of service, but when reward comes, it is a thing to be appreciated and savored. Only momentarily, however, for the next moment will bring another challenge. This is a summing up of administration in Academia.

A single achievement, stemming from a single challenge, can affect an entire institution; indeed, it can affect the totality of education if we stretch our minds to the furthermost. The widening concentric circles from a point of affirmative action or encouragement at the center are indicators of the impact and influence upon both close and distant constituencies. Who can imagine or measure the eventual positive effect of an accomplishment, however small or of little seeming importance on the scale of time? We can picture the relative magnitude of effect which ripples will have upon a chip of wood, a water bug, or a submerged stone or on a quiet pool into which a pebble has been dropped. Whether, at the outset, this is action of positive or negative significance for those affected, need not be considered; positive pebbles sometimes produce negative results. We can only hope that the influence will positively build and that the result will be of lasting and affirmative importance to the lives it touches.

The mind can quickly become boggled by the consideration of the crosscurrents and countercurrents which result when widening circles reach an unyielding point and are pushed back into the oncoming circles still emanating from the central influence. On the return trip, are they of positive or of negative nature? Is the turmoil they cause actually detrimental or might it be interpreted as supportive?

One thing seems certain: these actions and reactions can all be interpreted as potentials for achievement and as possibilities for reward.

Personal reward for an educational administrator is most often mirrored through his or her institution. Personal reward is most often quiet and simple. This seems wholly appropriate because we are not functioning for the purpose of "balancing out" hard work and recognition. Human nature allows us to be inwardly pleased with personal accomplishments. Is such reward enough?

There is no reason why the single institution or system which is our world of daily labor and concern should not take pride in accomplishment. The new chief administrative officer should quickly recognize that elements of good fortune, fertile and active minds of colleagues, and a strong personal motivation can always work together for the total and positive benefit *of the institution*. A sense of personal satisfaction coming out of having had a part in such total benefit ought to be reward enough. However, in spite of this rather missionary position on personal reward, there are elements at work which play upon it and which should be recognized. One should not feel a sense of guilt or a breach of humility when he or she is consumed by a sense of pride and reward. In the natural bond which exists between leader and institution, reward ought to be shared as readily as problem, search, and accomplishment. The test is put directly to the chief administrator. He must deal directly with manifestations of both personal and institutional reward and pride. His reflections of either need not be unenthusiastic nor of uncommonly humble posture.

Benefits Without Fringe

Always a thing of joy is good, solid accomplishment which occasionally emerges from an ocean of administrative junk. Another is when, all too infrequently, the fragments of a disjointed and distraught set of circumstances come together and hence into being as an entirely new educational entity. One is at times privileged to be present and attendant on such occasions and at such births.

Privilege is one of the rewards which we can periodically expect and to which we can look forward. Privilege of leadership is one of our benefits without fringe or fanfare. There are others.

There are helpful and loyal administrative colleagues; men and women of integrity, industry, and ability who are honest with themselves and honest with authority. Men and women who can put institutional advancement before personal ambition and who can develop their separate roles in a manner which will pull the parts of the whole together.

There are board members who have a keen appreciation for the basic purposes of the school or college which they serve without compensation. Not always in agreement with the chief executive, or with each other, but historically involved in the betterment of institutional policies for effective operation and long-range financial projection. And, in more recent years, deeply concerned about the totality of education so that financial decisions will have sound philosophical bases. Only those of us who have worked closely with such boards and with such individual board members can fully appreciate the extra benefit which this association has provided.

Another benefit without fringe is to be found among students who do not sit by and watch the institution drift or decay. We should be grateful for their growing perception and for their instant and unique reaction to potential or recognized weaknesses. It is students who can have the greatest enthusiasm for a school or college; it is also they who can be most troubled when institutional purpose and direction begin to stall or to reflect false promises. On most campuses, internal pulse and blood pressure are best determined by a cross section of student opinion. Rather than to discourage the taking of student pulse and blood pressure, we ought to welcome it and to increase its frequency. Student loyalty manifests itself in many ways, but the most important of these is criticism, because most of them *care enough* to be critical. This sort of student attitude can be of personal benefit to any chief administrator, if only he will view it as such.

Finally, and of equal major importance and benefit, are teachers who recognize that a full measure of academic life includes instruction, scholarship, and a sense of responsibility toward the young people with whom they are partners in learning. I am pointing to the teacher who feels a personal commitment to improve his or her teaching, who creates personal pressure for continuing and productive scholarship and who accepts the responsibility for optimum performance from each student. A faculty made up primarily of these sorts of teachers and persons is of real and tangible benefit to any principal or president.

When we anually ponder salary and fringe-benefit questions for our people and, after so doing, propose to provide increases and supplements wherever possible, there is an extra and essential exercise to be performed: the consideration of *the state* of our own continuing compensation. I am afraid that most of us fail to do an adequate job. Beyond the official salary and fringe benefits granted us, we need to total periodically the unofficial and fringeless benefits we enjoy: administrative and faculty colleagues, trustees, students, and a host of helpful and concerned constituents who, after all, make the difference between "holding a position" and "sharing in a challenging and rewarding life work."

Center Emphasis

The emphasis and thrust of institutional energies should be in direct relation to what we consider to be *centrally* important. We believe, or at least we spend a good deal of time saying so, that education must be people-centered. Most human institutions are, but especially, in education, which concerns itself with people-growth and people-building, the individual finds himself at the center of basic consideration. Authority and responsibility for the guarantee of center emphasis, in this case people emphasis, rests with the chief executive. This means much more than people-oriented programs and projects; it means more than an acute awareness of personal relationships with the subject people. It means a daily resolution and a complete daily dedication to the principle of putting teaching and learning first. This is not always easy to do. We expect that teachers, who are hired to put teaching first, will do so. We hope that students who are admitted or enrolled to learn will do so. But an administrator, who deals in absence slips, late registration, food service complaints, budget controls, parents with problem students, and students with problem parents is often hard put to remember that he passes himself off as "an educator."

The chief administrator is likely to be still further removed from the center of things (the educational process) unless he makes a daily and conscious effort to the contrary. A combination of factors has nearly eliminated his historical opportunity to teach which, if still possible, would be exceedingly good for him for a number of reasons. But there are other ways to be active at the center.

Administrative leadership can provide the environment, the money, and the enthusiastic support from the president's or principal's office so necessary to the center of educational activity. In return, the reward is active participation in the central role of any institution. Those "inside constituents" who sometimes verbalize the feeling that teaching and learning should be left to teachers and learners are quite right, but active involvement in the *whole of the process* need not be confined to the classroom. Satisfaction over a particularly good piece of work can and should be shared by those who prepared the ground and those who put the project into actual life and growth processes. The student-teacher-administrator climate in our schools and colleges is many times directly proportional to the amount of energy spent by each in a common endeavor. This concept, it seems to me, is of special note to the chief administrator as he moves within that climate.

From an "outside" position, the chief is called upon to interpret all campus goings-on to extra-campus constituencies. He is well advised to concentrate upon those things which are going on *at the center*. This is also reason for his own activity at the center for it affords the opportunity to tell the real story *as he knows it to be*. Without benefit of firsthand knowledge of the primary function and functioning of his or her own school or college, realistic interpretation is difficult and enthusiasm is impossible. What, we often ask ourselves, do parents, townspeople, friends, and former students want to know about the schools with which they have close connection and deep interest? Statistical information, in small dosage, is swallowable; graphic evidence of some sort of growth in physical plant, even if moderately administered, has a low threshold of tolerance. Plans for the future, even plans which capture the imagination, can be in time wearisome. "What is going on, *right now*, at the educational heart of my school or college?" is the question that needs answering for all groups on the outside looking in. (It might also be an appropriate question for some of those on the *inside* looking in.) The one person who is most called upon to answer that question cannot afford to know the least about it. A combination of being in, knowing of, and telling about the center emphasis is rewarding to all concerned.

Grasping and Reaching

The need to *reach* is, I think, an affirmative and confident need. One reaches for challenges, rather than waiting for them to come along. Indeed, challenges of any magnitude rarely appear to those who wait for them. Reaching is forward or upward, ahead of time, anticipating. Conversely, the need to *grasp* almost says "desperation" to me. It seems to be stretching backward or downward, in a desperate attempt to either hang on or climb back up. There is no doubt that all of us have done some grasping, or that all of our institutions have done some hanging on or some climbing out of a previous lower position, due to many factors either financial or educational. But in most of these instances would the grasping have been necessary if the power of reaching had been effectively used in the first place? Presidents and principals should be instruments of reach, of extension, of growing toward the next challenge to the extent of being almost anxious for it to arrive. To think and to perform in any lesser manner would be to reject the level of leadership which one's institution has every reason to expect.

The relationship of a chief educational administrator to his or her governing board can be affected greatly by the matter of reach versus grasp. In most instances, members of the board need to be reminded about such things as institutional reach, and it is the hired chief executive who must remind them. Members of the board, acting collectively or as individuals, should be able to share in the total and forward experience of the district, school, or college they have agreed to serve. The board itself needs to reach beyond the status quo, the expedient, the broad expanse of mere adequacy in education. Here, the chief administrator is a leader of yet another sort, not by usurping board authority or board prerogative but by opening the eyes of the board to continuing avenues of challenge and reward. This is rather like a call to vision, if the phrase is acceptable, a challenge in itself which should encourage a board to see beyond budgets and to reach beyond tradition and to share in the rich and rewarding experience of helping to move the total school or college forward and of knowing why.

The Continuing Challenge

There is always a new challenge, but there is always a new way to meet it; a new idea or a new pattern or a new concept. Think about that for a moment, or for that matter, think about it every morning. Consider the exchange of power between a challenge and an idea to meet it. Consider the relentless and natural replacement of problem with solution. This is not the exception: it is *the rule*. Challenges demand to be met, and there will always be ways of meeting them.

Presidential or principalian belief in the natural law of *continuing challenge and achievement* is perhaps the most important element in his or her professional consciousness. With belief comes confidence; with confidence comes strength; and with strength comes the reasonable and powerful enlightenment that educational growth and high purpose is not only possible but inevitable. It is not automatic, nor is it a calm and pleasant stream of orderly achievement. It is not likely that all within any institution can reach this level of understanding and accomplishment without the subtle strength and the overt encouragement of the chief executive. Reward, both for a school and its people, is tied directly to accomplishment and to share in accomplishment is to share in reward. The "why and when" of getting there is up to an entire institution; the "how" is the responsibility of the chief executive and is dependent upon his ability to lead.

If we remember that our primary charge is toward better education rather than merely better administration, the point of our task and of our leadership will be more clearly defined within the framework of continuing challenge. The total and inescapable responsibility for initiation of meeting and conquering whatever might stand in the way of enhancing the educational process is uniquely within the province of the chief administrative officer. He can meet the challenge alone or he can enlist the aid of others who believe, as he does, in the immeasurable potential for achievement. I am certain that we have all acted both singularly and in concert; different sets of circumstances demand different avenues of approach, but in *no way* and at *no time* can a principal, a superintendent, a president, or any institutional officer in final authority take a position of indifference or disinterest or rejection of the dictate to *move forward* to meet a challenge.

Always a Professional

Remember that those professional people who work with us are mindful that we are human and therefore fallible. Remember that they are human and therefore forgiving. Remember that we and they are most often mutually respectful. Remember that our profession needs a working philosophy and that work and philosophy are not strangers to one another.

Never forget that our students expect dignity, honesty, integrity, and candor, and that when they receive it, they usually return it readily and easily. Never forget that we uniquely hold the key to the inside and the mirror to the outside. Never forget that both our inside and our outside concentration must point to students and to the educational process. Our chosen profession is education, not administration.

No one else within the profession has the same broad measure of influence and prestige; we must use them wisely and with courage. No one else has the responsibility; we must use it from a position of personal strength and purpose for the benefit of institutional accomplishment. No one else has the sense of total opportunity and of total challenge; we must reach for them, and reach again, and yet again.

Reward is, at the same time, a challenge met and a challenge ahead. The chief administrator in education can be a credit to the profession only when he or she determines to settle for nothing less than to be at once and always professional. Reward is inherent in challenge and specific to task. Never-ending challenge and task is our way of life and we are privileged to serve in a profession of *life influence*. Let that be our challenge and, at the same time, our reward.

Second Thoughts

HAVING AT MY COMPLETE and private disposal about three hours in Honolulu between an appointment in the Bank of Hawaii Building and a banquet for Oahu alumni and parents, I reread and rereflected upon the thoughts expressed within the foregoing pages for the final time. Since one is seldom his best critic, there may have been no particular value for me then or for you now in an exercise of this sort, but several conditions were markedly different as I began this last critical look at what I thought that I thought about the strange and wonderful land of Academia and about the challenges and rewards afforded its chief administrative officers.

The first difference, a state of complete relaxation, was a feeling I had not experienced since the start of the academic year (and the start of the writing). Another was the knowledge that I had, even though not satisfied with all of the words and phrases, "let it all out," and that for me, reward had arrived no matter what the editors decided. Still another difference, perhaps most striking of all, was the view—something I had written a great deal about in terms of personal and institutional sight and insight. The view which now presented itself was a purple-turquoise-golden contrast to the black and brown and white southern Idaho winter which I had left behind. Second thoughts, in this rarified tropical atmosphere were difficult yet necessary. Unknowingly, I had stacked the deck; how could one have any but good thoughts or good second thoughts under the hau tree on the lanai at the Halekulani?

The essays are too repetitive, I thought. *They are too Pollyanna-positive. They make educational administration sound ultimately righteous, like one of the later Crusades.*

√ But, *I countered*, repetition can underscore a central theme, and here we certainly have a ringing central theme worthy of reinforcement.

√ And, so what if one's career makes him feel as if he is doing something affirmatively and totally worthwhile?

√ As for crusading, it may be past time for the *last* crusade. Where better to begin to fight it than at home? At home, where a positive, growing leadership will serve those students and colleagues whose assets and abilities are held in highest trust and regard.

The essays are intercontradictory, I worried. *They are too short. They are too long.*

√ But, *I argued*, the practice of the art of our profession is filled with contradiction, try as we might to be consistent. Indeed, contradiction, in its truest definitive sense, means *speaking out against*. The very soul of education is freedom to contradict and guarantee to argue. Such are not only very desirable, but also very necessary.

√ When is the written expression of one man's thoughts and concerns too long or too short? For himself, the question is unanswerable because the whirling and swirling in his own head never stops. For others, it can be too long after the first paragraph and too short after the last.

√ During this final reading, under the spell of sea, sun, and trade wind, the length of each essay or of the total collection did not really seem to matter as much as before. The reader ought to be able to arrive at his or her own conclusions without either my help or my apprehensions.

When the struggles and achievements of any institution or of its chief administrative officer are so very specific or personal, what is the point of sharing?

√ Not, surely, for purposes of advice or of counsel; each of us has his or her own membership card, and all are marked "nontransferable."

√ Not, I think, for purposes of impressing oneself or one's colleagues with the evidence that he has given a little extra thought and labor to the questions of what he is, what he is doing, and why.

√ These observations on creative educational administration, at first writing and at last reading, were a labor of love and of respect and of positive expectation toward the opportunities and challenges which will continue to greet us every morning of our personal, professional, and institutional lives.

√ What more can we ask than for opportunity and challenge? In themselves, they create the climate for accomplishment and reward. What more exciting career exists under the sun?

The challenges are beginning to stack up and I'm going to pack up and get on home. I've been away too long.